Aubrey De Vere

Proteus and Amadeus

A correspondence

Aubrey De Vere

Proteus and Amadeus
A correspondence

ISBN/EAN: 9783741193187

Manufactured in Europe, USA, Canada, Australia, Japa

Cover: Foto ©Andreas Hilbeck / pixelio.de

Manufactured and distributed by brebook publishing software (www.brebook.com)

Aubrey De Vere

Proteus and Amadeus

PROTEUS AND AMADEUS.

WORKS BY AUBREY DE VERE.

Alexander the Great. A Dramatic Poem. Small crown 8vo. Cloth, price 5s.

The Infant Bridal, and Other Poems. A New and Enlarged Edition. Fcap. 8vo. Cloth, price 7s. 6d.

The Legends of St Patrick, and other Poems. Small crown 8vo. Cloth, price 5s.

St Thomas of Canterbury. A Dramatic Poem. Large fcap. 8vo. Cloth, price 5s.

Antar and Zara: an Eastern Romance. INISFAIL and Other Poems, Meditative and Lyrical. Fcap. 8vo. Price 6s.

The Fall of Rora, the Search after Proserpine, and other Poems, Meditative and Lyrical. Fcap. 8vo. Price 6s.

C. KEGAN PAUL & Co., 1 PATERNOSTER SQUARE, LONDON.

PROTEUS AND AMADEUS:

A CORRESPONDENCE.

EDITED BY
AUBREY DE VERE.

LONDON:
C. KEGAN PAUL & CO., 1 PATERNOSTER SQUARE.
1878.

The Rights of Translation and of Reproduction are Reserved.

CONTENTS.

	PAGE
INTRODUCTION,	ix
PROLOGUE,	1

LETTER I.—PROTEUS TO AMADEUS.

Proteus answers one egotistical letter by another, and proposes "A Discussion." The danger of teaching people to think! He propounds a parable, . . 3

LETTER II.—PROTEUS TO AMADEUS.

Proteus proposes the questions for discussion. The portrait of a "Materialist malgré lui," . . . 7

LETTER III.—AMADEUS TO PROTEUS.

Amadeus enquires as to "Why he himself believes in a God?" A curious "religious experience." The evidence of God in Reason, Nature and Conscience, . 11

LETTER IV.—PROTEUS TO AMADEUS.

Intellectual sympathies of the disputants. The religious experiences of Proteus, ... 22

LETTER V.—PROTEUS TO AMADEUS.

Proteus considers that the evidences of God, in the inorganic world, have been weakened by the advance of Science. The argument of the "Watch." "Who made all this?" a question to be asked, not of Science, but of Theology, 31

LETTER V. (*continued*).—PROTEUS TO AMADEUS.

Proteus contends that the argument of Design in the Organic World is annulled by the doctrine of Evolution. Mr Darwin's theory. The mystery of the Beautiful. "Is there a purpose in the world of living things?" a question unanswered, save by Revealed Religion, 40

LETTER VI.—PROTEUS TO AMADEUS.

Proteus reviews the physical argument, and states certain objections against the moral government of God. "The alternative to which the rejection of God, the Creator, reduces me." He constructs the Matter-God, 51

LETTER VII.—AMADEUS TO PROTEUS.

A cryptograph decyphered. The "Riddle of the Universe." "It is IMPOSSIBLE there should not be a God!" "What is Law?" 59

LETTER VIII.—AMADEUS TO PROTEUS.

Amadeus declares that the doctrine of Evolution is neither inconsistent with design in Creation, nor at variance with Catholic doctrine. "The question of our Ancestry." 67

CONTENTS.

LETTER IX.—AMADEUS TO PROTEUS.

How Amadeus was affected on reading the "Origin of Species." Strong and weak points in the theory of Natural Selection. Three tests. The present stability of Organic forms. Certain questions of Proteus answered, ... 75

LETTER X.—AMADEUS TO PROTEUS.

Amadeus proves the existence of God from the instincts of animals, and shows the insufficiency of Natural Selection to account for them, ... 91

LETTER XI.—AMADEUS TO PROTEUS.

Amadeus discourses on the Beautiful, and the insufficiency of Natural Selection to account for it. Its account is God, ... 108

LETTER XII.—AMADEUS TO PROTEUS.

Evidences of the moral attributes of God. Why we should not look in the natural world for "mercy of a sentimental kind." The Future State. A boastful Postscript, 119

LETTER XIII.—AMADEUS TO PROTEUS.

Metaphysical and moral proofs of Immortality. The existence of a Future State a sufficient answer to objections as to the miseries of the present life, . . 127

LETTER XIV.—AMADEUS TO PROTEUS.

Amadeus a bad controversalist. He becomes the disciple of Proteus! Strange fecundity of Space, and a world self-created out of Nothing! The Matter-God in jeopardy. "How shall we shape our lives?"—Catastrophe! 137

LETTER XIV. (*continued*).—AMADEUS TO PROTEUS.

Amadeus reviews his argument, and concludes, . 153

LETTER XV.—PROTEUS TO AMADEUS.

Scepticism a disease of the soul. A cripple cured by fire. A picture of Hell. Wherein Proteus had been pleased, and wherein disappointed with Amadeus. The mutual relations of soul and body. A leaf out of Savarin's "Cookery Book." Proteus's hope of hereafter, not in the immortality of the soul, but in the resurrection of the body. The dizzy thought on God. He concludes, ... 160

INTRODUCTION.

THE same error assumes a different character, when it recurs in successive centuries. The Materialism of Hartley, a brief and profound refutation of which is to be found in the "Biographia Literaria" of Coleridge, once his ardent disciple, had apparently a purely metaphysical origin. Much of that which has lately asserted itself, has arisen probably from the bewildered though generous eagerness with which the young have watched the rapid progress of Physical Science. Physical Science has no more to do with metaphysics, than a piece of iron has with the north star; but if a piece of iron lies near the compass, that compass is deflected from the north. We are made up of habits; and where an intellectual disproportion has grown up, we dwell upon certain classes of thought to the disparagement of others, and exclusively apply favourite methods of reasoning to subjects to which they are but subordinately applicable. Insensibly some specific opinion, though in reality but an accident of our mental progress, acquires a masterdom over us, even while all that is highest within us, turns from it with distrust. Of this condition, the following correspondence is an example. "Proteus" comes forward as an apologist for Materialism, eloquent in its praise; while yet many an expression betrays the secret that his deeper sympathies are elsewhere; nay that he feels, though he does not know, that within the white outside there may be rottenness. His tone has nothing of the aggressive or the arrogant about it; it is marked on the contrary by earnestness and candour. That of "Amadeus" is equally free from controversial bitterness. It is like that of one who in conversation "thinks aloud," a habit which ever conciliates sympathy and trust. On both sides, not victory but truth, is sought. A character is thus imparted to the discussion which may well render it acceptable to enquirers. A correspondence which has arisen out of actual circumstance has, besides, one advantage over more elaborate works. It is less abstract and more real.

It would be unjust to assert that men of science have been generally hostile to Religion, though not more unjust than the converse allegation, viz., that the vindicators of Religion have been hostile to Science. Our most eminent men of Science, in late as in earlier days, have been Believers. There are unfortunately at present not a few exceptions;—moreover it is to be remembered that the recent popularization of Science has necessarily multiplied her camp-followers, a race more noisy and boastful than her soldiers. It is chiefly among these that we note a tendency to substitute the servile flatteries she despises for a reasonable service, and to undervalue all Truth except that particular sort of Truth which we gain for ourselves through discovery. Thus it sometimes happens, that when scientific principles themselves illustrate Religion and attest it, many do not observe the fact. Those who in the name of Science argue against miracles as injurious to the dignity of Law, (forgetting that "the exception proves the rule,") have also questioned the existence of a God, on the ground that physical suffering exists, suffering which, as "Amadeus" well remarks, could not have been banished from man's world of progress and probation, except by the substitution of special interferences innumerable for those Laws of Nature, in detail severe, though on the whole so conducive to happiness, without which both the virtues and the faculties of man must have lacked their training. Those who maintain that "Instinct" is "Reason" do not perceive that, on that hypothesis man would not stand, as they maintain, next akin to the ape, but find a nearer and worthier animal representative among the tribes of Ant and Bee, whose marvellous social polities are images of his own. Those who proclaim that all the countless species on the earth, from the lowest form of vegetable life to man, have been "evolved" from a common ancestor, of remote but very humble origin, often maintain, no less, that the various families of man are too dissimilar to have been derived from a single human stock. Those who are zealous about "Natural Selection," do not always observe that that principle has its bearings in connection with a great Doctrine of Revealed Religion. The "Survival of the fittest" means that, so long as life has been known to exist, it has been a warfare; and that to a death-struggle of ages hardly imaginable, animated nature owes whatever it has yet consummated of greatness or of beauty. But the Christian creed had also for nearly two thousand years affirmed the "Militant" condition of man; and proclaimed that that condition must precede his "Triumphant" state. The Christian *Idea* thus included the later philosophical one, and may well have suggested it to those who, as "Amadeus" and Mr Mivart have shewn, first thought of "Evolution," as the Law of animal life, viz., Fathers and Schoolmen, such as St Augustine and St Thomas Aquinas. Indeed, the Christian Idea had one advantage over the later application of it to "Species." The noble Warfare it announced, reconciled the interests of the Individual with the progress of the Race. Every soul, passing from Trial to Triumph, was both a pledge for the eventual Triumph of the Race, and a help to that end. The Human Kind was on an endless march towards perfection; but each successive generation had not long to wait for its "Golden Year." Those Fathers who first suggested "Evolution" as a possible interpretation of the Mosaic record, did not regard that theory as a Religious Revolution. Some thinkers who do thus regard it, and who have changed a theory into a creed perhaps a century before its truth can be proved or disproved, have reason to suspect their intellectual motives.

To disparage Science would be to dishonour one of God's greatest gifts to man. It is to her progress, and that of Liberty, that Humanity looks forward with most of confidence for her future:—but for their progress, nay for their permanence, it is necessary that Religion should maintain in the heart of each man, not only a place, but a power proportionate to the power wielded by its noblest rivals, and advancing with its advance. Only in one sense can Religion see an enemy in Science. Scientific truth cannot contradict religious truth, it is often said. Most true; but scientific error can contradict it; and the path of Science ever lies, through error, more or less partial, to truth. Before atmospheric pressure had become understood, it was philosophical to believe that "Nature abhorred a vacuum," and to add that her abhorrence extended only to that of a well thirty-two feet in depth. Science advances the more steadily for her victories being thus tardily won. In the meantime if the credulous acceptance of a scientific theory, eventually shewn to be erroneous, should cause the rejection of a single high religious truth by a single generation, the whole of Divine Truth, Natural Religion and Revealed alike, might thus be lost to the bulk of a nation—perhaps forever. Those who care *only* for Truth Discovered have minds too narrow for a serious appreciation of Truth. It is a larger thing than they know.

To the heedless, innumerable circumstances increase the danger at the present time. Archbishop Whately once remarked to me that, prolixity exercised a more deceptive influence than all the sophisms, classified in books of logic. In our day some ethical "non-sequitur," which would have been detected at once if compendiously stated, escapes confutation, because it is hidden in a work of three volumes. The bulk of the work is on Natural Philosophy; the reader is grateful for the manifold information it gives him, and unwarily swallows some moral or metaphysical inference, so false that it hardly affects demonstration. It is but implied; yet the assumption passes for a proof, because it is surrounded by grave scientific details of unquestionable value. A good table of contents might have exposed the fallacy.

Again, it is often taken for granted that an eminent

writer on Physical Science must be trustworthy in his metaphysical inferences. As well might we assume that a successful lawyer must be a natural philosopher. I have heard a man devoted to Science assert that the human race now existing, must have existed at least 50,000 years ago, on the ground that certain bones, exactly like human remains, had been discovered in a geological stratum dating back to that period. He could not be made to perceive that, even conceding the scientific part of his statement, he had unconsciously mixed with it a metaphysical inference for which he had attempted no proof. He had assumed first, that the bones could not have belonged to some animal race, since lost :—to such a race a bone-structure, far more like man's than the monkey's is, would not, even in the opinion of materialists, have imparted the human faculties, in the absence of a brain equal to the human brain. He had assumed, next, that the bones could not have belonged to a race, intellectual and spiritual indeed, but one whose course had been run before that of man had begun. On his hypothesis, viz., that during vast periods previous to the existence of man, as hitherto accepted, the earth was a fit habitation for races more than animal, and in body resembling man, the existence of such races, or their existence on earth after man's probation is over, would not be improbable. Many persons would say, "we think that the planets are inhabited, because otherwise vast tracts of space would exist in vain :— the waste of vast periods of Time in a single planet, would equally be a loss." To state these alternatives, *as possibilities* obvious to us, and as suggestive of other possibilities unknown to us, is consistent with reason. To affirm their negation, as *a fact*, is assumption. But men who despise metaphysics are always talking "fast" metaphysics without knowing it.

Materialism has moreover this allurement, that at its side are the *reiterated instances*, and those thoughts which carry an image with them. Material conditions alone cannot produce thought; yet material *conditions*, as well as *causes* derived from a far other source, are necessary for man's exercise of thought, so long as man has a body. Now, observing at every moment how much the intellect is affected by these bodily conditions, many persons confound the conditions with the causes; and repetition carries the day. Again, the apparent triumphs of matter address the senses as well as the mind; whereas the distinction between condition and cause addresses the mind only. Matter has thus an unfair advantage in its "dispute with spirit" —an advantage like that of an advocate, who intimidates by his vehemence, and seconds argument with gesture. Spirit, on the other hand, if it challenges us less often, and in a lower tone, approaches us with appeals of a deeper significance. A little book called "the Lost Senses," records the tale of a child called Laura Bridgeman, to whom of our five senses there remained but that of touch. When quite young she was sent to an Asylum for the Deaf and Dumb. Several years afterwards she was visited by her mother. By slow degrees she recognised certain touches of the hand to which she had been used of old when seated on that mother's knee. She was visibly troubled; gradually her emotion shook her more and more; at last she flung herself on her mother's neck. Few narratives are so affecting as this tale—one of many which prove how completely all our noblest faculties and affections exist in those who, so far as the senses are concerned, are immeasurably less endowed than the animal races. In such cases the affirmative proves everything ; the negative proves nothing.

The argument of "Amadeus" against the Materialistic Theory seems to me to have been everywhere urged alike with candour and success. He conclusively proves that Evolution, however easily the theory may be perverted, does not itself oppose Man's instinctive, and most reasonable recognition of a Divine design in Creation, since mere "Natural Selection" explains, not the *origin* of a species, but its *preservation;* the whole theory plainly leaving unsolved those three primary problems, viz., the first source of Matter, of Life, and of Law. His remarks on the Beauty of Creation regarded as a note of design are especially striking and original.

The scope of the whole discussion is necessarily determined by the conditions on which it was based. "Proteus" demands the evidence of Theism taken apart from Revelation. The condition surely is arbitrary, and less philosophical than it seems. Theism is doubtless *distinct* from Christianity ; but things distinct are not always separable. Genuine Theism ever included the hope of a Deliverer ; and historical Theism began with the promise of a Messiah. When Christianity became man's heritage it remained still the primal Theism, though developed and with the Promise fulfilled. It is by the link next the hand, not by the first link, that Humanity must take hold of the chain. In God Incarnate that Divine Image is palpably set forth which, to the mere Theist, was dimly adumbrated. Why should he who enquires after the original turn from the picture to the faint outline? To resemble the Theist of old times, we must, with Plato, turn our face to *all* the light accorded. It was Diogenes who shrunk from it into his tub. Had the higher Greek philosophers fancied that they could make religious philosophy "*Broader*" by making it include, not the largest number of deep thoughts, and high doctrines, which man had reached, but the smallest number only, viz., those in which all agreed, the Greek race in place of advancing to the acceptance of Christianity, must have receded to the condition of the barbaric races, which were "agnostic" in intelligence, respecting things divine, and, for that reason, idolatrous in their fancies.

We are indeed informed on the highest authority, that Reason is capable, even apart from Revelation, of knowing the primary truths of Theism. But—and it is important that enquirers should remember this— it does not follow that all Truth thus cognisable by man will be discovered by each individual man, no matter under what conditions he may choose to institute his search. If he discards the trodden road it is not certain on that account that his strength and skill will carry him to his journey's end, even though practicable bye-paths through the jungle unquestionably exist. The Copernican System is a thing discoverable by the human mind: it has actually been discovered; and the knowledge of it has made its way, by the help of authority and of good sense to the unlearned. It is not to be inferred that any particular individual, no matter how high his talents, who chose to renounce provisionally all scientific authority, and all methods of thought except such as he had himself selected, would be able to re-discover the Copernican System. The same difficulty may arise in our enquiries respecting the primary truths of Theism, if we let go what was once ours by inheritance. However, if the conditions of discussion prescribed by "Proteus" are undesirably restricted, that circumstance, though it leaves the discussion incomplete, detracts nothing from the importance of what has here been done. The subject is vast; and each part of it has to be treated. Many readers will hope that it may be resumed hereafter; and that the remaining portion of it may be treated with the same ability, freedom, and friendliness, which characterise the discussion laid before us.

Such a supplement would have the closest affinity with the enquiries already here recorded. In Revealed Religion we learn, not only the true character of that God announced by Theism, but also the true character of man's being, and consequently the nature of those conditions, moral and spiritual, without which his intellectual energies, setting up by themselves, in separation from his total being, can learn of God, perhaps not much more than an intelligent domesticated animal learns of Man. If the intellect needs bodily conditions for its external work, philosophy might well anticipate what to some philosophers seems a scandal, viz., that it may need, not less, the recognition of certain *spiritual* conditions, when grappling with its highest themes. The allegiance of the lower to the higher, in man's nature, is at least as natural as that of the higher to the lower. The moral and spiritual conditions under which alone, (this is the very hypothesis of

Revelation), Religion consents to impart to the human Intellect, the highest part of its dowry, constitute a subject which would need a volume at least as large as the present. Those conditions include most of the virtues, the manlier as well as the tenderer, and chiefly Humility. This is what Science might have been the first to anticipate, since she begins with the same demands. The man of Science addresses the man of the Senses with a warning that there is no "pride of knowledge" which is not exceeded by "a greater pride" of ignorance. He says to him in the words of St Augustine, '"so receive these things that you may deserve to understand them." You assure me that you see the sun move, and feel that the earth stands still. Be not too confident. You are mistaken in both particulars. Science appeals from the senses alone to the senses *co-operating* with a higher power: and the greatest of scientific men said he was "a child on the sea-shore picking up pebbles."' It does not seem less reasonable that Religion should say, "There is a third region higher yet than those two of the senses, and of science; and its apparent contradictions are apparent only. It has mysteries *because* it is Religion, and deals with the Infinite in the interest of man's Spirit. Let the Reason, in union with those senses, to which it has taught the advantages of a noble subordination, look forth upon larger worlds, through the telescope of Faith. This is *not* to close her eyes." Such is the doctrine of the Newtons and the Bacons. It will remain for ever attested by Bacon's "Student's Prayer,"[*]

---

[*] To God the Father, God the Word, God the Spirit, we pour forth most humble and hearty supplications; that He, remembering the

the reproach of too many who claim to be his heirs, but are not his sons.

As regards the lesser men of Science, some of whom not only doubt, but deny, a God, one cannot help thinking what a stir would be made by one of them if—*Theism having never been heard of before*—he had himself just begun to grope after the discovery, but through appliances exclusively scientific; marvel after marvel, and mystery after mystery, and attribute after attribute, dawning slowly upon microscope or spectroscope!

In these days, when so many destined for greater things are unwilling sceptics for a time, it may be well to call two things to remembrance. The first is that, though Religious Belief is *certainty*, not probable opinion, it is not a certainty based on mathematical deduction, which would destroy its moral worth, but a certainty not less absolute and more vital, based on the joint action of Faith and Reason. The second is that, if all things are disputable, this arises not because all things are doubtful, but because the versatility of the human mind is endless. An argument for and against the existence of an exterior universe, or even as to Personal Identity, might, if

calamities of mankind, and the pilgrimage of this our life, in which we wear out days few and evil, would please to open to us new refreshments out of the fountain of His goodness, for the alleviating of our miseries. This also we humbly and earnestly beg, that human things may not prejudice such as are divine; neither that 'from the unlocking of the gates of sense, and the kindling of a greater natural light, anything of incredulity, or intellectual night, may arise in our mind towards divine mysteries. But rather that by our mind, thoroughly cleansed and purged from fancy and vanities, and yet subject and perfectly given up to the divine oracles, there may be given unto Faith the things that are Faith's. *Amen.*

the opponents were equally matched, be carried on, like a game of "Cat's Cradle," for all time. Eventually we have to decide to what part of our mental and moral being we will trust ourselves; in what part of it we will dwell; on its heights, or in some suburb, or "Ghetto."

A. DE V.

CORRESPONDENCE.

PROLOGUE.

AMADEUS and PROTEUS, some twenty years ago, were together at College, in the relation of MASTER and PUPIL; but subsequently, divided by their respective fortunes in life, they lost sight of one another; though, meantime, the remembrance of an intercourse which had ripened into friendship was mutually cherished during the years of their separation. At length, in the summer of the year 1876, the long silence was broken by an interchange of letters between the two friends; and, at the suggestion of Proteus, that discussion, or controversy, was commenced, as to the momentous truths of the Existence of God and the human Soul, which furnishes the matter of these pages.

The controversy once ended, the friends met. Then Proteus, in the hope that a discussion which had greatly benefited himself might be useful to others, urged the publication of his friend's letters, and when Amadeus would only accede to this request on the condition that Proteus himself would also make public his own portion in the controversy, the latter with great reluctance consented.

Indeed, such reluctance was shared, though not perhaps to the same degree, by both writers; and its motive will be appreciated at once by the reader of their letters. That spontaneous quality, which constitutes the main charm of an epistolary style, would be lost if the matter were carefully elaborated for the Press. And besides, it had to be made with them, so to speak, "a rule of the game" that what was once written should stand, or merely verbal alteration be allowed; so that the bad argument could not be mended, the random statement revoked, nor the untenable position altered for a better one. No wonder then, if, upon both sides, there are failures to be acknowledged. But such matters—provided only the beneficial result proposed in the publication were, on the whole, attained—would be mere trifles.

There was more, in truth, at stake than a mere matter of personal vanity. That sacred *egoism*, which is the life and soul of a letter, the generous interchange of friendly confidences,—even the secret whisperings of God in the heart, and the wounds of a soul estranged from Him, were to be submitted to the cold scrutiny of the stranger! for they are made to enter largely into the argument. It was obvious that a strict *incognito* was the only means of escape from the inconvenience of the method which the writers had adopted. Indeed, they are disposed to ask, if it may not be permitted them, in such a case, to assert a privilege, which has been awkwardly claimed by previous writers in a similar position,[*] that, viz., of disowning the authorship, if challenged on the subject in a spirit of curiosity?

To the same intent, fictitious names, for real persons and places have been adopted throughout. A.

---

[*] Thus, Sir W. Scott, questioned about the authorship of *Waverley*, is reported to have answered, that he was *not* the author, but that his answer would be the same, supposing he were. Sir Philip Francis, when challenged by a lady, as to the authorship of *Junius*, replied, "Do you mean to insult me, Madam!"—A.

LETTER I.

PROTEUS TO AMADEUS.

Proteus answers one egotistical letter by another, and proposes "A Discussion." The danger of teaching people to think! He propounds a Parable.

MY DEAR AMADEUS,—Your letter found me in the midst of troubles and vexations, such as you have fortunately no experience of, and it has consoled me not a little. Its "egotism" was more delightful to me than a world of kind inquiries could have been, for it proved that you still had faith in my affection. I am astonished when I think of it, and remember that twenty years have gone by since we met, without word or sign from me. How shall I thank you? I suppose, as the beggars do when you have given them a meal, and who ask for sixpence, by asking for something more. I am encouraged to propose that, as we are not to meet this year, we shall at least correspond, and that our letters, if you will, shall take the form of a discussion.

Now you must know that I hold you responsible for certain intellectual errors into which I have fallen, and indirectly, for much of the misery of an illspent life. It was you who first taught me to think, and surely *thought* is at the root of all evil. It has occurred to me that you ought to feel remorse for this, and to find it a relief to your conscience to do something towards saving a soul you have brought so near perdition.

The fact is I am just now at that point in life where, the fever and the fret of youth being mostly spent, I am looking round me for some means of making a composition with my soul's creditors, and resettling the little that is left to me of my intellectual estate. I want a pretext for thinking over again certain propositions, once familiar to me, but long ago abandoned as hopelessly barren, and this time, if possible, towards a different result; and I want a companion, for I cannot face the idea of setting out again alone upon such an enterprise, knowing as I do the vicious circle I should tread, the maze where thought abandoned me twelve years ago. Will you go with me here, and be once more my guide and philosopher, as well as friend?

Of course! I am sure that you will do it, that is if time and strength permit. But, who knows, you may be prevented in a thousand ways. You may be out of health or out of heart, or simply too busy to attend to me. Still, if you feel something of the fire of other days, and have the leisure for such a work, I will make bold to lay before you my position on certain fundamental questions, involving life and death to my soul, and ask you to throw the light of Christian philosophy upon it. You will inquire, "Am I sincere in what I propose, and is it my will to be convinced; or am I not rather one of the scribes and pharisees putting vain questions only to be answered in vain?" To this I can but say that, without professing full faith in the result, at least I am prepared to consider it the greatest piece of luck that can befall me, if it is proved that I have been deluded, the sport of an evil dream.

I will make a parable:

There was a young man, the son of a great lord, and heir to a great estate, who, tempted of the devil, or his own vanity, and having access to the muniment room in his father's castle, looked one day into the box which held the title deeds and registers of his descent. Of these the young man found that some were missing, others obscure or tampered with, and some again which cast suspicion on his birth. In deep concern, and troubled by this doubt, he goes to the family lawyer, a prudent man, who shakes his head, assures him that his claim will never be disputed, and bids him hold his tongue, and enjoy without more ado the property, as soon as it shall be his. But the young man is too unhappy for this, and with the mystery uncleared refuses to take again his place as son and heir. Then, having argued all the case, and become convinced that he is in truth no nobleman's heir, but a gipsy's son, he leaves his home for ever, and his name and titles and his father's roof, and seeks to gain an unhappy living by telling fortunes and stealing fowls.

He goes from bad to worse, and is brought at last to justice. Then, as he sits upon the prison floor, loaded with chains, and with his own bitter thoughts for company, he sees how grievously he has erred, throwing his life away, and bewails his folly. To have been content with ignorance had been better wisdom ; but how undo the past, how force back faith to its old channels, and believe again in his lost estate? Then too (may I say it?) in his distress a wise man comes, an expert, a reader of genealogical riddles, a decypherer of manuscripts. The missing papers are restored. The registers shewn to be a forgery, and the young man, restored in blood, and proved once more to be the son of a lord, is let out of prison, (for such is the custom of the country), and lives an honest life happy for ever after.

All which means that I would give everything I possess for a reasonable excuse to abandon reason, or better still, to find a cure for my madness in reason itself, a hair of the dog that bit me. Here is egotism in return for yours. Oh that you were with me this July weather, that we might talk of all things in heaven and earth under these trees!—Yours affectionately, PROTEUS.

LETTER II.

PROTEUS TO AMADEUS.

Proteus proposes the questions for discussion. The portrait of a " Materialist malgré lui."

MY DEAR AMADEUS,—Since you have given me leave to speak, I will proceed to state my case, premising only that you must be patient with me if I appear to halt in argument. I have read little during the last dozen years, and my logic and metaphysics are almost forgotten with disuse. I was never more than an ignoramus in theology. You must treat me, I am afraid, not at all as a philosopher, even in the Crowhurst sense,* but as that thing philosophers most despise, a man of the world, remembering too that the object of our discussions is not that I should be refuted but convinced. I say this now less for the purpose of covering a possible retreat than that you may not later on be disappointed in finding me a fencer unworthy of your steel. But these explanations are after all of the nature of "*les coquetteries de l'esprit*," and I cut them short.

The questions that I would propose for our discussion are these:

1*st.* Is there a reasonable probability (apart from

---
* At Crowhurst, a student in the class of philosophy was called "a philosopher" a divinity student, in the same way was "a divine."—A.

the teaching of the Church), of the existence of a personal God, just and merciful, who rules the world? And

2nd. What are our chances of a future life?

Very old questions surely, which have been put a thousand times, and have been a thousand times answered, but none the less new for that to each individual mind which comes into the world. We believe, but why do we believe, or we doubt and why do we doubt? We all have to ask ourselves this. To me individually the two questions I have proposed are still full of obscurity and terror, and still require an answer. The position of doubters in the present day is no longer met by the text books, and materialism as now expounded by the Royal Society was certainly untouched by your philosophy class of twenty years ago. That I am a materialist you must be prepared for, a materialist, that is, in argument, but not (believe me) in sympathy. Indeed, this quarrel between my beliefs and my desires is what galls me more than all else in my position. If I could fall in love with unbelief as many do, I should be happier, and perhaps should find comfort in a martyrdom for Truth's sake; but as I see her now she is too unlovely. No:

> "Truth is a harlot who has sold her wares
> To all the world, and each in turn declares
> His knowledge that she came to him a maid,
> And for that fact would jeopardise his head
> And as one day he goes to death for it,
> He sees Truth walking naked in the street
> With a new lover. Will that man admire,
> Think you, the simpleness of Truth's attire
> I tell you he will spit upon her face

And bid her home to clothe her nakedness
In any falsehood.—I had rather dream
The dream the shepherds dreamt at Bethlehem,
Than solve for ever the world's theorem
And find Truth nothing."

But alas, it is not a question of wishing, or of taste, or of feeling. In all these I am a Catholic, and I cling to the name with an almost superstitious fondness. The Church, as an institution, is to me a venerable and a noble thing, and I have a true filial feeling towards its supreme Head. I am not of those who would take umbrage at the nickname of Ultramontanism, having no sympathy with any school in the church but that of Rome. As for heretics, Jansenists and freethinkers, if I be one of them, I do not love them. Bismarck and Garibaldi are to me as personal enemies who have done me a wrong; and I should rejoice to see the triumph of the Church by arms in Italy. I revere the Jesuits, who in part educated me, and Father Carter still stands first in memory among my patron saints. On the other hand, neither Mill, Spencer, nor Huxley inspire me with the least enthusiasm. I am as thorough a disbeliever in the perfectibility of the human race, by means of State education in physical science, as any *monsignore* at Rome. In a word, I have every claim to be ranked among "*les bien pensans*," except that of belief. Why then do I not believe? No. If it had been a case of wishing I should not now be where I am; but alas, the wish is not always father to the thought, or the thought grows up an unruly child, and forces itself upon our will with irresistible power. Like Death, Winter, the Germans, and other repulsive assertions of power, materialism must be counted with by all who acknowledge the logic of facts. It is fearful to think that there may be no God, and fearful to think that we may die wholly in death; yet it cannot be a question of what is good or bad, beautiful or fearful, but of what is true or false.

It is surely no warp in a mind that compels it to ask this. Be patient with me then. I am a materialist but "*bien malgré moi*;" and my sympathy with the things of darkness is only the sympathy of despair. But we must be children indeed to repeat the cry, "These things are too terrible. They cannot be true."

I reserve the opening of my argument for another letter; or will you not rather speak first?—Yours affectionately, PROTEUS.

LETTER III.

AMADEUS TO PROTEUS.

*Amadeus enquires as to " Why he himself believes in a God ?"
A curious " religious experience." The evidence of God in
Reason, Nature and Conscience.*

MY DEAR PROTEUS.—If I have been long in answering your letter, it is because I did not care to take up your case till I felt I could give my whole mind to it. How gladly I would be of service to you, and, if possible, convince you that you are no " changeling," but lawful heir to the *estate!* And indeed I trust, ere long, to see you in possession.

I will remember your cautions; that I am not to be too subtle and metaphysical, but practical, and that I am not to refute, but to convince you. This latter condition suits me well. I often boast that I am the worst controversialist in England; for I never yet knew a man to be refuted into anything.

But I confess that the task is a very difficult one, and I hardly know how to set about it. One man's mental complexion differs so much from another's, that arguments which seem all-powerful to some have no weight with another class of thinkers. And yet, unless we really strive to put ourselves in our neighbour's position and look at things as he looks at them, no good can come of discussion. I am going to ask you, then, in answer to your question as to the existence of God, to weigh the motives which induce *me* to believe (setting aside the authority of the Church) in a supreme Being. If I say anything to good purpose, use it, and may it profit you; but if you think anything in my argument be inconclusive, do not trouble yourself to refute it, but simply put it on one side. And I, on the other hand, will endeavour to understand your case, and explore with you that Cavern of Despair which is your present abode; though I cannot conceive how you got in there. That it is no pleasant place to live in no one feels more keenly than yourself. But enough of tropes, and *in medias res!*

The question is, is there a reasonable probability (apart from the teaching of the Church) that there is a personal God, just and merciful, who rules the world?

Now, although the existence of a supreme Being is borne upon the common mind with overwhelming force, yet the argument is of a cumulative nature, and it is hardly doing justice to it to criticise it piecemeal. Any one argument, taken by itself, does not compass the whole conclusion. Hence the proofs are not so overpowering as they ought to be, to one who does not consider their cumulative force, but regards them one by one.

Newman, (I forget to what purpose) alludes in his Grammar of Assent, to the difficulty of proving, in a manner equivalent to the strength of our conviction, that Great Britain is an island. And yet a man would as soon doubt that twice two make four, as doubt that fact. And elsewhere, the same writer says, that he believes in a God for the same reason that he believes in his own existence, though he has never been able to throw the argument into mood and figure to his satisfaction. I should think not indeed. I may say that I believe in a God as certainly as if I saw Him; but if I were asked to state the grounds of this belief, they are so manifold and various that I do not know how to start. I feel that my very hesitation will count against me. It is an "*embarras de richesses;*" what ought to be my strength is my weakness, and I fear to lapse into vague generalities.

In default of logical order, then, I will have recourse to the order of events. I propose to examine my own mind, and find out how, in *me*, the belief in God originated and has developed. This sort of egotism is not odious; it is oftentimes necessary. A man can examine no other *ego* than his own.

Now of course, when a child, I was taught that there was a God, and I took it on faith that they told me truly. But I am sure that this does not account for my belief now. I have out-grown the influence of many teachers, and never found any difficulty in divesting myself of opinions taught me by them, as often as I discovered these to be false. But of this belief I cannot rid myself. I could not do so without doing violence to my nature. *It is human to believe in a God*; and the common voice of mankind is with me in this matter.

My early education, then, does not account for the belief. Here is the account of it.

The first argument for the existence of God came into my mind when I was very young (I could not have been more than seven years old). I remember it well, from a circumstance attending it which stamped it in my memory. But of course, I could not have set the argument in words, or called it by name, which was this, "*There must be God or nothingness.*" The conviction came, and like a lightning-flash it *scared* me. I was like the moth which has come too near the light and gets its wings singed. Mind, I believe I am describing, not a mere state of mind, but an objective fact. The force of the argument I can appreciate now, but I cannot *reproduce* the token which accompanied it, for I never *produced* it. I firmly believed that it was a token sent by God as His *Bené* to the argument. But if you choose to set it down to the credit of my imagination, of course you are free to do so; I have heard others speak of similar experiences, so I daresay the phenomenon is common enough.

Now as to the argument itself. It is at the bottom of many of the school proofs, into which I shall not enter further than to indicate them, such as, "If ever there was an epoch when there was nothing, there would be nothing now: there must therefore be an Eternal, necessary Being as the foundation of reality." Then there is the argument of causation, which is nearly related to, if not another form only of the same argument, about which I only want to say this; that if it be logically faulty, as Kant supposes, there must be something wrong in the statement of it. "If there must be a cause for all things *what is the cause of God?*" argues, I think, more wit than wisdom on the part of the querist.

For surely the very theory of causation implies a first cause; else there would be neither causes nor effects. However, let that pass. I don't think that any reasonable being can deny that there must be a necessary Eternal Being, as the foundation of reality. I have got no further than that as a matter of argument. The result would be meagre enough if the argument stood by itself: For here is no God, in our sense of the word, but only a necessary Eternal somewhat; and even if I add that such a Being must be infinite, since there is nothing to limit it, I have still no definite object of apprehension. But I have allowed that no *single* argument will compass the existence of God.

When I began to read, as a boy, I soon fell in with the argument of Design—Paley's argument; but I knew nothing about Paley then. The argument is plain to the understanding of every child, and points the moral to many an early reading lesson. It is the practical, common-sense argument, roughly stated in the words of Napoleon.: "You may talk as much as you please, gentlemen, but who made all that?" (pointing to the starry heavens). Or, in other words, Creation exhibits every where manifest marks of design; and design is unintelligible without a mind; therefore the world has an intelligent Author.

Kant could not deny the force of the argument, as thus stated. But if I remember rightly, he objects to it that it does not give the *technical* conception of God. Exactly: it fails to give a self-existent, Eternal Being; but the metaphysical argument has supplied that defect already. So soon as my reason tells me that there must be a self-existent, Eternal Being, as the foundation of reality, I look into the visible world, and what do I see there? Such a work, surely, as is only worthy of such a Being. The bare statement of the argument, as that contrivance argues a contriver, hardly does justice to it. In the Psalms the God of Nature is considered not merely as Maker, but as Thinker, as Artist. "Thou hast multiplied Thy wonderful works, and in *Thy thoughts* there is none like to Thee." "God is the Lord of knowledges; for Him *thoughts* are prepared." "I will meditate on all Thy works, and be employed about Thy *inventions*."

I will dwell on this aspect of the case, because you enquire, not as to an essence, or force, or substance, but about a *personal* God. A person is *individual, iutelligent* and *free*. Now there is just this character about the works of Creation that manifests its Creator to be personal. His work is the work of an individual mind, as opposed to mere machine work, which strikes out a number of objects all moulded to a fixed pattern. Look at the some hundred and fifty varieties of humming-bird, and the some four hundred and fifty varieties of the fern tribe. How He seems to revel in the infinite resources of His inventiveness! How many countless variations of melody in one simple theme, in this Divine Artist! What curious choice of means to meet the multitudinous circumstances in which the different tribes of birds, beasts, and insects are placed, that they may live and thrive! And then, as if this were not enough to manifest that it is a living, personal Agent, He caricatures, so to speak, His own types, in such fancy work as the rhinoceros-beetle, the humming-bird moth, the monkey, the parrot, and that waxen plant with waxen flowers, which appears, as it were, the imitation of an imitation! Nor does this view of the matter seem to me irreverent; but rather it is a sweet attribute of the Almighty, that He should in His works sometimes appeal to that sense of humour with which it pleased Him to endow the minds of men. Hence the Divine Wisdom (personified) exclaims: "I was with Him forming all things, and was *delighted* every day, *sporting* before him at all times, *playing* in the world; and my delight is to be with the children of men," Prov. viii. If then the God of Nature be not personal, I must be at fault as to what personality means; God is personal if Turner or Beethoven be personal.

This view of the case absolutely silences, to my thinking, a dark suspicion that sneaks into the mind when we merely consider the metaphysical argument. "Perhaps the Universe itself is the necessary, Eternal Being, which is its own account; perhaps all that exists, necessarily exists; perhaps all things are only so many infinitely various evolutions of One necessary, Eternal, infinite, somewhat, substance, unknowable, what you will!" With this sort of talk I find it difficult to keep patience, seeing what the work of Creation really is. I could as soon believe that a sonnet could compose itself, or a landscape paint itself, or a poem write itself, as I could believe that God and Nature are the same thing.

When I got technically educated in natural Theology, I don't think it added anything to the force of my conviction that there was a God. It would have mattered little to me, as far as the conviction was concerned, if the school-proofs had turned out to be mere sophisms. They helped to *regulate* my thought of the Divine Being; they taught me to know Him better, but the conviction had not its root there. Where had it its root then? In my conscience.

If my teachers taught me that there was a God, I

might have given to the statement a mere notional assent; I should have taken what they said to be true, but should hardly have realized its truth, except for my conscience. There I found Him whom they told me about. If, again, I learnt to realise the existence of God, from the argument of design; yet I might have been strangely perplexed about the moral attributes of such a Being, except for my conscience. For the argument of design solves the great mystery of the origin of things only to start a multitude of other problems. Whence is evil, loss, defect, blight, a heavy yoke upon the children of men, tears and pain, and that king of terrors, Death? Is God good, merciful, just, holy? My conscience tells me that He has always been a good God to *me*. For, if my heart warmed sweetly within me, whensoever I acted worthily of Him; if it were wrung with the bitterness of fire when I have acted basely, I never doubted but He put that there. No doubt then, He is a just and merciful God who frowns so darkly on my injustices, and cuts me so to the quick when I am less than merciful to my fellow men. He is good and holy who thus humbles and confounds my unholiness, and puts my naughtiness to shame; and again, when I repent me, and seek Him, catches me back again into His bosom and the sunshine of His love.

But then, if God be good, why is the world so out of joint? This was the problem of the gloomiest of the Prophets. "Just, O Lord, art Thou when I plead with Thee. Nevertheless of justice will I speak with Thee. Why doth the way of the wicked prosper?" Yes, and why are the good oftentimes trampled upon and persecuted? How do I answer that? Well, I admit that it is a disadvantage to me that I cannot argue here like a Christian. However, on one point I take my stand, and it is enough. Since God is good to *me* of His own good-nature (for what advantage can He get from me?) I doubt not but He is good in Himself, and to others, *if only I had before me the whole state of the case.*

I do not want to argue with Him about His judgments, like Jeremias, for I know I am but a child in His sight. When He won me to love Him, He won me to *trust Him.* Let the existence of evil stand over until I know more about it. Love can endure this and many other problems. As far as evil comes near myself, I do not repine. If I have suffered, it has been to my unspeakable good. I should never have known half His love and worth, except for my own miseries. And so I doubt not, it will be with the crown of agony—Death. I have ever seen His finger in the conduct of my life. He has ever laid a gentle hand on me, and I will trust Him to the end.

But, if any one should say that conscience is not the voice of God in my breast; that it is only an acute sense of disapprobation; that it is a reflexion in us, of the voice of society; that it is our better self condemning our worse self; I must say as Hume says, laughing in his sleeve (of another matter however), "Perhaps they are right, perhaps they are differently constituted from me in this respect." The account is miserably inadequate to explain the fact. I know what fear of exposure is, or dread of public opinion, and I fancy the most hardened criminal has it, but is that conscience? Such a feeling is merely subjective; but, about the visitation of God in the breast

He lets us know by unmistakeable tokens, that it is He, and that He is wroth. The fact of conscience is objective as well as subjective. But it would seem if a man should deny this, I don't know how to cure him. I know that conscience is like the alarum-bell, with which a man is awaked in the morning; if he do not hear and obey, it ceases to rouse him, and as they say of such a one, "He has no conscience." But it would be uncharitable to think so of any individual, unless I know that he is a bad man.

There is another account. A man may get a warp in his mind by over-working a single tendency. If he should overwork the speculative reason, for instance, it might be to the injury of the practical. So perhaps a metaphysician is not the best person in the world to consult about so eminently a practical matter as conscience.

And now, dear Proteus, I have answered your question as well as I can. I say that *there is more than " a reasonable probability that there is a God;"* but less convincing reasons would satisfy a loving heart, because *Credula res amor est.*

For my part, could I be brought really to disbelieve that there is God, I would not wish to live another day. I do not find this world so passing sweet that I should care to linger on, till stone, or gout, or fever, or asthma broke up this machine of the body. The highest good in this life, short of God, is the love of our fellow-beings; but love is very poor and helpless, and where it is closest it is not all-satisfying, because there is an infinite craving in the heart of man which only God can satisfy. There are times in a man's life when God comes so close to him that he cries, "It is enough!" But I never felt this of the love of any human being, De Vere says the same,:—

> "Vainly strives the soul to mingle
> With a being of our kind;
> Vainly heart with heart is twined,
> For the deepest still is single.
> An impalpable resistance
> Holds like natures still at distance;
> Mortal, love that Holy One,
> Or be for aye *alone.*"

Dear Proteus, Affectionately yours, AMADEUS.

LETTER IV.

PROTEUS TO AMADEUS.

Intellectual sympathies of the disputants. The religious experiences of Proteus.

MY DEAR AMADEUS,—Surely it is a token of much intellectual sympathy, in addition to the sympathy of heart which your letter proves so clearly, that even in the arrangement of our discussion we should have adopted the same order and method. In a letter which I had written, but did not send you, I also had begun with a sketch of my spiritual life; and, as a second point, I had proposed to ask you your own experience, and to compare it with certain recorded experiences, such as are shewn in the lives of the saints and Bible history. My third point was to be the evidence of God's presence in the material universe; and my fourth the metaphysical argument. Is not this almost exactly as you have treated it?

I begin then, as you have begun, with my experience of God in my own heart, and this is what I find: I do not remember realising any of the "truths of religion," before I was twelve years old, or having felt seriously my relations with the unseen world,* till I was prepared for my first communion by the

* I was not taught as a child to think about ghosts; and, though cowardly enough when alone or in the dark, it was nothing spiritual that I feared, but robbers, wolves, snakes, and other material fancies.—P.

Jesuits at Ravenswood. Before that time I had cared nothing for the things of the spirit, nor had I understood them. I was by nature affectionate and truthful, but otherwise my disposition was not a noble one. I was idle, greedy, selfish. I was without ambition, shunned labour, had no self esteem or desire of distinction, enjoyed amusements which did not involve trouble or exertion, and placed my ideal of happiness, if ideal I had, within the four walls of a kitchen garden. I had no special love of mischief for mischief's sake and none whatever of goodness. Indifferent health had led to my having been rather spoiled at home; but my education had been a careful one, and I had no special temptations to evil.

I take it that mine was a fair sample of ordinary human nature, neither good nor bad, merely selfish. From this state of lethargy, I was roused by Father Carter, for whom I first conceived an admiration as something greater and better than myself, and worthy of imitation. He seemed interested in me, had me caned once or twice, and won my affection. To please him I became a good boy. I made a spiritual retreat, and I then discovered for the first time, as a reality, the scheme of God's government of the world. I learned that this life was only a preparation for another life, and, with the alternative of heaven and hell before me, I was logical enough to see that the future was the only one worth living for. At that time I vividly felt God's presence as a reality in my daily occupations. I did my best to please Him; but I do not remember that any special token of this presence was given me such as you describe, still less such as one reads of in the lives of the saints.

I was only six months at Ravenswood; but I am convinced that, if I had remained there, the influence I have described would have lasted. Perhaps I might now have been a Jesuit. But I was taken away from that school and sent to Crowhurst. You know what Crowhurst was in our day, —a place without religious colour of any kind, a sort of "Sleepy Hollow," where nobody was quite wide enough awake to be vicious. It suited my natural indolence to a most unfortunate degree; and, though I continued to be a "good boy," it was without intelligence, and without fervour.

I felt however the want of something more; and, though I ate and drank, and slept to my heart's content, I was not satisfied. Religion at Crowhurst was unattractive. Its representatives among ourselves, the church boys, were, for the most part, coarse and rampant. Dr Winterton, the president, preached all his sermons on holiday afternoons, and bored us accordingly. Our best type of asceticism was the excellent Canon Marlow. The soul cried out for more; and at last more was provided. You came to Crowhurst; and I think George and I were nearly the first of your disciples. You gave us the spiritual food for which we longed, though in a different form from what I had found it at Ravenswood. You taught us to think, to reason, to argue. As Father Carter had been my spiritual so you became my intellectual father; and, where he had based the truths of religion on the heart, you built them up to a more imposing structure in the intelligence. The Jesuits were afraid of reason. I remember their suppressing a little volume sent to me by my mother in which the motto occurred, "Through the contemplation of created things, by steps we may ascend to God." I have since come to think that they were right. But you had no such scruples. You showed us God in His works, in the necessities of the human mind, in the metaphysical contradictions involved by a denial of Him. At that time I believed, with the most implicit faith, that not only were the truths of religion reducible to absolute mathematical certainty, but that true reason could not do otherwise than fortify and illuminate our belief in them. I think I had no suspicion at that time that its sword could ever turn in my hand against myself. With these ideas, and a taste for discussion, but with no very profound knowledge either of theology or metaphysics, I went into the world.

I was then sixteen; and for two years I can note no particular change in either my belief or my practice of religion. I was fond of the innocent pleasures of the world. My friends were not vicious, nor had I much temptation to vice. I regulated my conduct on the ordinary rules of the church teaching, and, if not an enthusiastic, I was at least a conscientious Catholic. I then went abroad to the embassy at Constantinople, where, in spite of my being thrown almost entirely with the ungodly, I persevered for a year and a half in the practice of religion, lukewarmly perhaps, but still conscientiously. I began however to find my religious profession, even among Catholics, in many ways irksome; more so than I should find it at the present day; for in early youth there are few things which a sensitive person feels more keenly than any singularity, whether it is of person or mind, or even of dress.

The only people of my friends who professed religious convictions were certain Swiss Protestants, who, without entering into any sort of controversy with me, shewed me another phase of religious belief and obedience to conscience. I was surprised to hear these persons talking of "the grace of God, spiritual experiences and theological convictions," in the identical language used by Catholics, and yet with certain fundamental differences of dogma, which made it difficult to believe them affected, either by the grace of God or by a true religious experience. And here I think, unconsciously, I found myself face to face with the first great difficulty which besets an inquiry into the rival claims of faith and reason, namely the existence of more faiths than one. But this is a subject I will not enlarge on now.

I returned to England in the autumn of 1860, restless and dissatisfied. I felt a craving for more knowledge; and, although I still had conscientious scruples with regard to a certain class of reading professedly irreligious, I devoured eagerly much miscellaneous infidelity, such as one finds in newspapers and magazines. I was sorry for such indulgence afterwards, and confessed it regularly, as a sin. Early in the following year, I, being then between twenty and twenty-one years old, was sent to Germany, and there came into direct contact with professed doubters and unbelievers. Those with whom I was thrown by my position discussed these subjects daily; and you will understand the necessity I soon felt for fuller instruction of one sort or the other. I was still hopeful, if not quite confident, that a better understanding of the questions affecting me would result in a complete reestablishment of my religious beliefs. But it is most difficult for an ingenuous mind to rest satisfied with only one side of an argument, or to argue with an absolute "*parti pris*" which no result may affect.

Feeling that it was no longer possible for me to resist the temptation of a full indulgence in the reading I desired, I wrote to my confessor in England, to ask him to get permission for me to do as I wished. He answered that he could give me no such permission; and I nevertheless read such books as "Essays and Reviews," the "Vestiges of Creation," and "Darwin's Origin of Species," the last a work which had more influence over me than any other in forming my opinions. My reading these books under these cirstances was, I think, the first deliberate sin I ever committed; and the result was soon apparent. I became more than ever dissatisfied. I began to doubt where before I had only been perplexed, and I neglected many of the duties of my religion. I was very unhappy, perhaps more unhappy than I have since been, or ever can be again. The ground was crumbling under my feet, and I saw a bottomless abyss beneath me. As with you, I saw the alternative of God or nothingness, and I was, as you were, appalled. I still however believed enough to be greatly frightened at my state of mortal sin, and I was continually expecting to die and suffer eternal punishment in consequence. I dared not, during the whole of one winter, ride across country, for fear of breaking my neck, or did so with fear and trembling.

This state of things lasted with me for the better part

of a year; and was brought to a crisis by a letter I received from my sister, saying she intended to become a nun. She was my only sister, and the person I cared most for in the world; and the prospect of losing her acted on me like a challenge. I felt that, before submitting to such a loss, I must know the truth of what was being done. I went to England, took my sister away from the convent, and arranged that she should put off her intention for two years, till she should be of age. But the first blow had been struck, and I was now at war with God. I abandoned the practice of religion, and, though still leading a moral life, indulged without reserve in my intellectual debauch; and before long, from looking on God as my enemy, I began to disbelieve in His existence altogether. I was still however more and more unhappy. I was not all at once ready to console myself for the loss of God and of a future life with the pleasures of the world.

My last effort on the side of belief was a retreat I made in the Redemptorist house at Clapham, in the summer of 18—, which I felt would be a final test. I agreed to dismiss, for the time being, all discussion and all the claims of reason. I made a general confession, and my heart was acted upon almost to the point of submission; but I was still, at the last moment, unable to say, "I believe." I read St Augustine's "Confessions" there, and sought in vain for a sign, for a voice in the garden; but no voice came. I left my retreat with unavailing sorrow, and set myself to enjoy the present life as best I might. I had a severe illness in 18—, during which I was nursed, and for a time converted, by a Sister of Charity; but on recovering, in the autumn of that year, I fell in love, and began to lead an immoral life. Since then I have hardly had, even for an instant, the consolation of a doubt.

I suppose, you can scarcely conceive the state of a mind which sees only with the eyes of the body, which looks at the earth by day, and the moon and the stars by night, and sees no mind, no consciousness, no meaning in the universe. I have never, even in a dream, heard the voice of God, or seen a sign of His presence in the world. As long as I was in love my love sufficed me, and I cannot say, as you do, that no human love ever satisfied the desires of my soul. I have, on more than one occasion, seemed for days together to be walking some cubits high above the ground; and certainly, during the whole of that time, some three years, I did not think of or regret the loss of religion. As I told you however in my first letter, I am no longer satisfied with anything that the world can give. I have during the last few years had once more a strong desire to believe. My enmity to God has long ceased, and I would fain make my peace with Him. But still the same darkness encloses me. I cannot find God. I cannot say "I believe." I have entered into this long history so as to make you understand me when I say, "There is no feeling in my soul of the existence of a being with whom she spiritually can converse, or whom she can believe to be listening to her prayers." I am then, I think, without internal evidence on which to start in my search for God. Where else shall I find Him?

In my next, I will treat more directly the subject of

your own most delightful letter; but I will not put off sending this now, for fear you should think me ungrateful. Indeed it is not so,—Yours affectionately,
PROTEUS.

⁎ *A letter of Proteus is here omitted, as the subject of it has been considered out of the main line of argument. It treated of miracles, answers to prayer, God's dealings with mankind, and the rest.*

LETTER V.

PROTEUS TO AMADEUS.

Proteus considers that the evidences of God, in the inorganic world, have been weakened by the advance of science. The argument of the " Watch." " Who made all this ? " a question to be asked, not of science, but of Theology.

MY DEAR AMADEUS,—Next to the evidence of God's presence, in our own hearts and in the hearts of others, you have placed the testimony of the material universe. I know that this has generally been held to be conclusive, and, at a certain stage in the history of human knowledge, perhaps rightly so ; indeed even so lately as in the age of Voltaire, it was no doubt rash to reject it ; but little as I believe in the real progress of human intelligence, viewed as a whole, I cannot but see that, in the particular matter of physical science, its knowledge has made a gigantic stride within the last hundred years. So much so that, where the Church was then easily victorious, a new battle has now to be fought with the same enemy, but in far different force. Balmes, in his "Letters to a Sceptic," which I have just been reading for the first time, and for which I avow an unbounded admiration, evades a battle with science, on the ground that there is too little union among its teachers to make a contest necessary. He leaves them, as it were, to cut each others' throats, and turns his sword with terrible effect on enemies of another kind. I wish he had not done so; for Physical Science is the only real giant of modern times and was the one most worthy of his steel.

I would not have you suppose me, however, an enthusiast for this branch of knowledge. I am too much of an artist by nature to feel a special sympathy with the mechanical details of the universe. It does not interest me to know that the speed of a falling stone is increased according to geometrical proportion, except in as far as such a fact may indicate a mental process in nature; and even the more congenial examination of organic forms does not commend itself, as such, to my mind. I have however been deeply interested in the great doctrine which the present century has produced, and which every new discovery made during the last fifty years has confirmed and exemplified until it is difficult not to accept it as a law, as absolute as that which Newton and his age discovered,—I mean the doctrine of evolution.

This, if true, (and to me it bears the stamp of truth far more distinctly than the law of gravitation) has indeed been a discovery of transcendant importance; for it is the solution of the chief riddle of the earth, the existence of man. I think that, in the presence of such a doctrine, it would be unwise to rely entirely on the proofs of God's action in the material universe which sufficed our fathers. I do not say that proofs cannot still be found, but there is no longer that absolute dilemma—"Whence has man come? From the bowels of the earth? If so, who brought him hence, himself or another?" The inorganic world indeed remains unchanged; but its arguments are weakened with the weakness of its ally, the world of life, if it has not already laid down its arms. You must not think that I have never been touched by the majesty of the heavens. I shall not easily forget the night on which my mother, walking with me in the garden at Walton, first spoke to me of the stars, and explained to me that they were not the mere twinkling points of light they seemed, but suns and worlds as large as ours, but far away, and having their laws and courses in the sky. It needed little argument of hers, in the face of that immensity, to make me repeat that only God could have contrived, or could comprehend, so wonderful a work. God was already to me a familiar thought; and the suggestion of His name was a pleasant and natural refuge from the bewilderment of this new vision. Yet which was in truth the more vast, the more incomprehensible, the more bewildering of the two? For one who has lost the sense of the reality of God's presence in the world, the thought of him is no longer a refuge; it is only an additional mystery added to the mystery before his eyes. The stars have since then become to me a stumbling block and a reproach in my search after God—a reproach because they seem to say, "Are we not infinite, all-powerful, eternal enough, that you ask for more?"—a stumbling block, because they add, "And you have sought a meaning for that which has no meaning, a cause for that which is without cause, a mind for that which has no need of mind." But enough of this for the present. Let us look at the heavens once more, and see if we can discern in them the working of a mind.

I see that Balmes approves very highly his sceptic's

comparison (not a new one) of the celestial mechanism with the mechanism of his watch; and perhaps it will keep us from generalities (which are often perplexing), if we follow out the similitude, and examine its worth. I begin as the sceptic (in this instance no sceptic) did. I take out my watch, a respectable family timepiece, with a double gold case: and I try to examine it as if I had never seen a watch before, and was called upon to decide whether it was a natural production or a work of man.

At first it seems as if it might be either. It seems alive. I can hear its heart beating, and yet it is unlike any creature I have seen before. It is cold; it is motionless. It is made of quite different substances from any I have met in the composition of organic beings. At the same time, it is evidently something more than a lump of gold. I look at its face, and find as its main features, a large and a small circle, either of which is marked at exactly equal distances on the disc with 12, we will say unknown signs; the twelve intervening spaces being in turn marked off, each with five points. There are two hands attached to the larger circle, and one little one to the smaller. On examining closely, I observe that the larger of the two principal hands makes its revolution round the circumference exactly twelve times as fast as the smaller one; while the little hand of the smaller circle revolves exactly sixty times as fast as the faster of the two first. Here is mathematical proportion which I have been accustomed to consider a mental process.

I go further. With some difficulty I succeed in opening the works, and I observe what first appears an elaborate but meaningless apparatus of wheels, chains, springs and cylinders. All I can understand of it is that their motion seems to be connected with the motion of the hands outside. On inspection, however, I find that the diameter of one wheel is just three times that of a second; that there are just twelve times as many cogs to this as to that; and it is not difficult for me to imagine that there exists a certain mathematical proportion everywhere. I find moreover, that the wheels revolve on pivots, of ruby apparently, as being the point most exposed to wear; and that there is a certain variety of material for which I can conjecture a corresponding advantage. I am also struck with the general neatness and finish of the whole thing; with some agreeable flourishes round the keyhole; and especially with the likeness of a rose, with flowers, leaves, and thorns, engraved on the plate which covers the movement, and the legend "by the King's patent," and the maker's name. I feel more than half convinced that the thing is a work of human intelligence; for I have recognised several of the mind's chief characteristics—mathematical proportion —the choice of means to an end, beauty of design, pictorial imitation, and if you will, handwriting, legible or illegible. Of these the first and the last, especially distinguish the watch from any known production of nature, and suggest a human origin; while the others, though less particularly characteristic of mental action, are not without their weight. Lastly, I set myself to discover a purpose in all this complicated machinery; for I admit that no reasonable being would have been at such expense of thought and labour, without an adequate object. The beauty of the toy is hardly sufficient to account for the pains bestowed on it. I feel the necessity of a *reasonable purpose*. Perhaps I am not able to guess it: or perhaps, after observing carefully the movement of the hands, I notice that two revolutions of the hour hand coincide with the space of time between sunrise and sunrise. It is near the equinox, and I connect the first revolution with day, the second with night. The purpose of the mechanism has become apparent. It is an instrument for marking time.

I think you will admit that I have stated this fairly, although you will be inclined to attach equal weight to the evidence of choice of substance, beauty of design and pictorial imitation with that of mathematical process. But you must remember that I have been set to distinguish a work of human intelligence from a "work of nature," and that organic nature shews an apparent choice of means, an apparent sense of beauty, and a few apparently conscious imitations. A discussion of this point would, however, be foreign to our immediate argument (which of course lies in the application of the same system of examination to the celestial bodies); but I will not shirk the existence of beauty, adaptation of means and the rest, when we come to an examination of the organic world. I therefore proceed—

The heavens show us an indefinite number of stars. Those visible to the naked eye having been computed at from three to six thousand, if we do not include the irregular line of the milky way, and the nebulæ of the southern hemisphere; and I do not know that any definite shape or system has ever been attempted to be given them; though it has been stated that our earth is near a centre, of which the milky way should be the circumference, of the solar system. We know more. I find it, according to general authority, to consist of the sun, and, besides other bodies, of the following planets, whose size, distance from, and period of revolution round the sun, I have put in tabular form thus:—

	Diameter in Miles.	Dist. from Sun in millions of Miles.	Period of Revolution round Sun.	Round Axis.
The Sun,	880,000	0	0	25½ days
Mercury,	...	36	88 days	24 hours
Venus,	7,700	68	225 days	nearly 24 hours
Earth, 1 Moon,	7,926	96	365 & fract	24 hours
Mars,	4,100	142	687 days	25 hours
About 30 small planets,		mean distance abt. 250.	about 1500 days	
Jupiter, 4 Moons,	90,000	485	nearly 12 years	10 hours
Saturn, 8 Moons, 1 ring,	79,000	890	29½ years	10½ hrs.
Uranus, 8 Moons,	34,500	1800	84 years	9½ hours
Neptune, 1 or 2 Moons, 1 ring,	42,000	nearly 3000	about 165 years	.

Besides these, which revolve in circles round the sun, there are comets whose orbit is elliptical, and whose revolutions round the sun are very various, and whose numbers and laws are little known, and also innumerable meteoric bodies still less understood.

In all this system, in spite of a certain uniformity of motion, it is difficult to discern a distinct mathematical conception. In shape most of the bodies are spheres; and all seem to approach the spherical form, as if by the result of a common force upon a common substance. We may liken them to the pebbles on the sea shore. That they have a common substance also seems proved; and astronomers have very plausibly assigned them a common origin from a single mass. The heavens, moreover, from our point of view, shew no trace of pictorial imitation, in spite of the fanciful shapes attributed to the constellations; still less is there anywhere the hand-writing of their maker distinguishable to our eyes. Lastly, but not leastly, what sign of purpose is there in this multiplicity of globes, with their endless revolutions or their endless fixity? Who has suggested any other than that of our dear "Uncle Toby," that Almighty God had willed it to be so?

It requires all our faith in the destiny of man to imagine a meaning for these countless bodies of fire. In themselves they present no meaning, no purpose, no design. On every side we see action, but not intelligent action. Even such purpose as may be conceived, for instance in the law of gravitation, is distinctly an unintelligent purpose; for though a stone may, at first sight, seem to have a purpose in the persistence of its attraction to the earth, yet, if by moving a hair's breadth to right or left, it would find a passage to the earth's centre, it will not move. It has no reasoning choice of means. It acts blindly, unconsciously.

I will not multiply instances. Perhaps in the whole range of this inorganic world, there is nothing which could be taken for the direct result of a mental process, unless it should be certain crystals which conform to mathematical rule. Napoleon may well ask "Who made all this?" but he should ask it of theology, not of science.

I therefore submit, though not dogmatically, that there is little or no real evidence of mind in the material inorganic universe—of mind at all analogous to ours—and if not analogous to ours, by what signs shall we know it? for surely it is a *petitio principii* (if I use the term rightly) to say "God's reason is not our reason, His justice not our justice, His mind not our mind"—I reserve, though I have already written it, the continuance of this line of argument as applied to the organic world for another post.

(To be continued.)

LETTER V. *(continued.)*

PROTEUS TO AMADEUS.

Proteus contends that the argument of Design in the Organic World is annulled by the doctrine of Evolution. Mr Darwin's theory. The mystery of the Beautiful. "Is there a purpose in the world of living things?" a question unanswered, save by Revealed Religion.

HITHERTO we have considered only the world of matter in its simpler form of unconscious forces; but there remains another world, which is as a garment to the first, of far more complex texture, and subject to a far more intricate law, the organic world, the world of life.

If, as I think, the argument of God's presence based on an examination of the one must have always (the psalms of David notwithstanding) been logically weak, that suggested by the other was clear till yesterday, and without an answer. You have touched already on some of its strongest features, the uniformity in variety of structure, the subtle adaptation of means to ends, the richness of invention, the beauty of form and colour, even the sportiveness of fancy in imitation and caricature. All these you have indicated as suggestive of a mind at work, of a mind delighted with its own power and its own creation.

It is an ungracious task not to admit the fulness of such reasoning; and I confess that, if it can be shewn that evolution is a baseless fabric, void of credibility, I will throw science to the winds, and worship God in nature as David and our fathers did. If it were not for the explanation, so clearly given by modern science, of nature's action in the organic world, I should hold the single fact of uniform structure in the skeletons of birds, beasts, and fishes, conclusive evidence of a mind at work, of a designer, of a God. But the question is changed. It is no longer an intellectual alternative between accident and design, but a physical problem susceptible of historic proof. The mystery has been explained by a law; and the argument based upon a dilemma of reason vanishes. Thus, it is an ascertained law, (that is the statement of a constant fact) that, in organic nature, "like produces like," or rather, "like with a difference." We know this historically, and I think you will hardly argue special design from the likeness existing between two brothers, or, on the other hand, from the differences they may display.

If then this rule be extended to the converse, "Like is produced by like with a difference," what do we gather from similarity of structure (as between birds and beasts), but that there is consanguinity? and if consanguinity how design? I think the burden of proof is thrown on those who would shew that there is not consanguinity in structural resemblance. On the other hand, the fact that resemblance is not perfect cannot be made to prove that there is no relationship; for brothers are not perfectly alike, and yet we have historical evidence that they are related. If however it can be shewn that resemblance exists where there is no consanguinity, and if no other law can be cited in account for it, and if the cases are numerous and clear, then we may fairly appeal from mere material forces to conscious imitation and design.

The instances you have cited of the rhinoceros-beetle, the hummingbird-moth, and I will add the leaf-butterfly, and the stick-caterpillar, are cases in point. The rhinoceros-beetle I do not know; but let us consider the moth, which I know well, as I do its double, the hummingbird. Of course no Darwinian, however zealous, would deduce the resemblance here found to any blood relationship; but it is not unaccountable on other grounds. In the first place, the likeness between the animals, if you examine them in your hand, is not striking, and is of course at all times quite superficial. The shape of the four wings of the moth is only vaguely like that of the two wings of the bird; and the resemblance between them lies principally in the tails. But, when hovering at the mouth of the flower, the motion of the wings and the impetuous movements of the moth are the same as the bird's, while his proboscis seems to imitate the other's beak. The movement of the hummingbird-moth however is not greatly different from that of other sphinx moths, while the hummingbird himself differs widely from the rest of his kind.

Of the two, therefore, it would be fairer to say that the bird imitates the moth. But I think it is not necessary to suppose any imitation. The habits of the two are the same, their wants and their way of satisfying them the same; and a rapid motion of the wings, and an expansion of the tail is necessary to either, in order to sustain itself stationary before the flower. I have purposely avoided alluding in this instance to the evolutionist doctrine of adaptation of form to circumstances, as it hardly seems to require it. As a fisherman, you must have often noticed bats and swallows flying together at dusk with so exactly similar a flight that you could not tell them apart. The reason is obvious. They are both catching flies, and are obliged to adopt the same manœuvres in the pursuit. The case of the butterfly which when alighted resembles a leaf is much more striking, and requires an explanation in Darwin's law. Still stronger to my mind is that of the bee-orchis, which is difficult to explain on any theory. Indeed I will confess at once that the whole question of the strange variety and beauty of the flowers is one which I have not yet had answered to my satisfaction. So many exceptions, however, have in the event proved the rule of natural development that this too is not improbably destined to become a proof.

I have been taking it for granted all along that you are well acquainted with the leading features of the doctrine of Evolution. But perhaps, as Balmes did, you may have despised science too profoundly to examine its arguments.

I will therefore in a few words sum up its principles as I understand them, and as I should conceive them carried to their ultimate results. An evolutionist would therefore no doubt say that matter, under certain chemical conditions not yet understood, has at some previous time acquired, if it may not still be acquiring, in addition to its ordinary qualities of extension, resistance, heat, motion, and the rest, a new accidental quality called life. I cannot think that it is necessary for belief that he should understand the exact manner in which this has taken place, any more than it is to understand precisely how heat suddenly bursts into flame. Indeed the transition from no life into life is probably less startling than that from darkness into light; for the change, in the former instance, is so gradual that there are many substances about which we are still in doubt whether they are organisms or not. That in the earlier stages of life there is development seems incontestable; but, I fancy, it is extremely doubtful whether the power of reproduction was at once acquired. I take it that many rudimentary organisms have come into being without any such power; though, as far as I know, all those we know of as now existing have it. However acquired, this power once established, the rest seems easy of comprehension. Any minute variations in the circumstances of reproduction would seem naturally enough to account for corresponding variations in the forms reproduced.

Hence little by little, circumstances being necessarily different in different cases, different varieties of rudimentary organisms have shewn themselves. And here Darwin, who lays no claim to the discovery of the principle of evolution, a principle known for the better part of a century, supplies us with a law which, from its extreme simplicity and exact fitness for the circumstances to which it has to be applied, bears the stamp of a true law, that is, of the statement of a constant natural fact. This law is known as natural selection, through the survival of the fittest in the struggle for life—or, to explain it more fully: The world has not room for all the beings that are born in it; hence a struggle for life ensues, and those best adapted for the struggle tread down those worse provided. The survivors reproduce their kind (for like breeds like) with their advantages.

Hence the advantages are permanently acquired. This, I think, in a few words, is the doctrine of evolution and Darwin's law, both so simple in character and logical in form that, if they could be applied to the lower forms of organic life only, it is probable the world would have been of one mind as to their value—but a greater issue than theirs was at stake, and the corollary of man's relationship with the beasts was not hard to draw. On Balmes' principle of "quod nimis probat nihil probat," the law has been rejected by half the world, not on its intrinsic merits. For my own part, though not in any way a lover of science, I have travelled much and observed much, and, although it is now nearly fifteen years since I became acquainted with this law, all that I have seen has corroborated and exemplified it, with the single exception I have mentioned of the variety and beauty of the flowers.

This, though not a contradiction, is in appearance an exception to the rule, which requires that each beauty or advantage in an individual should be not for the benefit of others but of the individual itself. I should be glad to find Darwin's law plainly in fault, and still more glad to find it reconcilable with the teaching of the Catholic Church. It is however, believe me, a power which must be counted with, and either overthrown or taken into service by the Church; and it is idle to count it for mere folly. I have watched the growth of its acceptance from the first appearance of the "Origin of Species," from the day when the *Edinburgh* and *Quarterly Reviews* disdained even to understand the nature of its argument, to the present, when I find it accepted by three out of four people I meet, and by nearly all the scientific world.

But this is too long a digression, and we must go back.

When we were endeavouring to identify the action of mind in the mechanism of the watch, one of the principal tokens of its presence was the mathematical proportion observable in the arrangements. Is there anything analogous to this in the mechanism of the organic world? I think, on the contrary, the mathematical element is conspicuous by its absence. I can hardly think of any instance, unless it be the coincidence of our having ten toes and ten fingers. The double organs seem essential to the proper balance of the body; and that the teeth in the two jaws should correspond in number seems also a necessity. I observe no mathematical proportion in the number of petals or stamens of the flowers. The number of leaves on any given tree is probably not the same as on his neighbours, nor in any distinct mathematical proportion with theirs. Can you suggest anything on this head?

Of adaptation of means to an end there are of course innumerable instances, though probably few of an absolute selection of substance, such as we found in the watch; the best example would be the lime of which the shells of the shell-fish are composed. That the adaptation is in reality a reasoned selection, and, as such, a mental action, will be doubted by all who hold the doctrine of evolution. Nature would seem to work as the ivy does in getting through a wall.

There may be only one chink in the wall and that a tortuous one, yet the ivy will find it. At first this would seem a mental process, but it is not so. The ivy has no stronger mental faculties than other plants, but succeeds by the nature of its growth, which pushes this way and that into every chink, and against every stone, and so at last into the particular chink which is passable.

Is not this a type of all natural process in the adaptation of means to an end? Can you give me an instance of a natural organ which has the features of a reasoned choice of means? or of anything analogous to pictorial imitation? As children we used to see an oak tree drawn in the section of a stalk of fern; but the likeness was doubtful. The ball-and-socket ornament on the peacock's tail, which seems to be shaded by design, has been treated of at length by Darwin; but, as a general rule, it is remarkable, with all its beauty, how little imitation of other natural objects there is in the variously pencilled plumage of the birds. Whenever there is imitation the corresponding advantage shews itself close at hand; and, as in the case of those creatures which resemble the ground they inhabit, it is less the sportiveness of caricature we recognise than a stern law of necessity and the struggle for life. Of true pictorial fancy I cannot recall an instance besides the death's-head moth.

And now we come to the subject of beauty, which I have promised not to shirk, while I own myself in the presence of a mystery. Why is the world beautiful to us as a whole, and why are certain things in it more beautiful than others without a corresponding advantage to ourselves? That there is an absolute beauty, independent of the eyes, the ears and the other organs of sense, no materialist will admit; and it would seem impossible to define beauty otherwise than as that which is agreeable to our senses. But why are they agreeable? If there were in all cases a corresponding advantage with the beauty of the object a reason would not be far to find. Our senses would be an instinct of what to seek and what to avoid. To a certain extent they are so. Our horror at the sight of certain reptiles is a warning which has its distinct advantage; and I have noticed a similar emotion in the monkeys, our near relations, whose only dangerous enemies are snakes. There are some funguses too, and poisonous plants, which fill us with repugnance, and without doubt our sense of smell teaches us to avoid decayed matter which we might otherwise eat. It is a distinct advantage that the smell of excreted matter is especially loathsome to us.

On the other hand, bright fruits attract our eyes; the edible mushroom has a pleasant smell, a woman's voice delights us. But for one instance which supports there are twenty which contradict the theory of advantage. Is the bitter sea less clear than the river? Are poisonous berries less red than the rest? Are all things sweet and pleasant good for food? Do we find the dead beast on which we prey as beautiful as the beast in life? Is the tiger an ugly thing? I think this theory of beauty cannot be maintained. Why then do we find the world beautiful? Is it by some law of inherited sympathy that, when the peacock displays to me his gorgeous train, and rustles with his wings till every plume of his body shivers, I feel the magnetism of his beauty as the hen before him does? I see the advantage of his beauty to himself, (to the fascination of his plumage he owes his very existence), but how to me? and, if it is sympathy, why am I not affected by the red-rumped apes, in whom I acknowledge far closer ties of blood. Still less, what have I in common with the flowers that they fill me with delight? Are they even conscious of their own beauty? I perhaps alone of all creatures find the oak tree a majestic thing. The trees, the grass, the flowers themselves have lived in blindness from all time, and die without so much as a guess at their own loveliness. All this is a riddle to me, which no Darwin has yet read.

Have we then here at last caught God in His retreat? Has God eyes like mine, that He sees beauty where I see it; ears like mine, to hear delightful sounds; a tongue to taste sweetness; a scent, that He should know the rose from the carnation; a touch, that He should enjoy the delights of sense? I cannot understand it, as I cannot understand why the sky is blue to me—the grass green.

There remains to ask, Is there a purpose in the world of living things?—an end, a design, in all this life—this reproduction, this decay? Of individual purpose the world is full. Each creature that has breath seeks to maintain his little being; his purpose is clear. But what of a general purpose, of a conscious will working through all these consciousnesses towards a definite end? The history of the world of living things has been but a long succession of creatures which have been born and died, of races which have grown up and disappeared. Was there a purpose once for the dragon and the behemoth, that their place knows them no more?

What is the reason of the races which devour and of the races which are devoured? What shall be the end? I can find no answer to these questions out of Revealed Religion. The sun arises and sets, the seasons come and go, the winds rage, the tides ebb, the moon wanes and is full; and all that lives upon the surface of the earth and in the sea makes its best of the winds, and the tides, and the seasons, or is destroyed by them. Each individual there has a purpose, his own life; but Nature reveals no purpose. It cares as little for the destruction of a race as for the destruction of a single soul. Even man himself, who in the last wonderful transformation of Nature stands, as it were, a god upon Nature's neck, is there a purpose in his life, in the tears of his childhood, in the folly of his youth, in the little wisdom of his riper years, and in the idiotcy of his old age? No, none in the world visible to the eyes of sense; or why should he struggle for a world to come?—Your affectionate PROTEUS.

LETTER VI.

PROTEUS TO AMADEUS.

Proteus reviews the physical argument, and states certain objections against the moral government of God. "The alternative to which the rejection of God, the Creator, reduces me." He constructs the Matter-God.

MY DEAR AMADEUS,—Now to review our evidence, and, if possible, to point to a conclusion. We have examined the physical universe; and I think that I have succeeded in shewing, first, that there is no distinct mental process discernible in inorganic Nature, and, secondly, that, in organic Nature, its presence depends upon our rejection of the law of evolution. I am willing to rest the issue on this point, although I consider that the negative evidence in the first case is a strong presumption against any affirmative evidence in the second, especially if taken in conjunction with the general want of purpose which I discern in either world. It would certainly be a remarkable fact that in a vast universe the display of distinct reasoning process should have been reserved for so insignificant a part of it as are the living creatures on this world's surface, and that they alone of all created things should have merited an elaborate design; and if such a fact could be shewn, a corollary might be fairly drawn of the peculiar value of the organic part of creation, and, as a further consequence, of that of its supreme feature, man; whence, in natural order, the chief doctrines of revealed religion would follow.* It seems to me, therefore, of the utmost importance, that this matter should rest on secure grounds; but the burden of proof should lie, surely, with the advocate of reasoning design in the organic world; for this would have become the exception, not the rule, of the universe.

For the rest, our discovery of uniform action in the forces of matter is inconclusive of design; for if, as materialists believe, matter is the eternal necessary being, it cannot be surprising that it should have eternal, necessary conditions of existence, its way of being or, if I may so call it, its "modus vivendi." I doubt even if it is possible to realise distinctively the classical idea of chaos, of matter without law. The fact that material forces can be stated according to a mathematical formula is only expressing in another way the statement that they are uniform. The same may be said of what has been called the law of compensation, in which some have seen the elements of divine justice, as when violent exertion is followed by sleep. This is no more than the action and reaction of forces. Even beauty, which, as I have said, is the enigma of the world, seems to be a condition of matter which our senses have learned to appreciate, as they have learned to appreciate heat and cold. For, in as much as all material objects are beautiful from some

* This is a remarkable passage. It is a confession that to deny the existence of Design in the material creation is (apart from all question respecting God) to deny all greatness to Humanity; and 2dly, that to concede Design is to accept, implicitly, not only Theism, but the "chief doctrines of Revealed Religion."—*Ed.*

one or other point of view, and to some one or other pair of eyes, beauty seems to be inseparably connected with matter, and is not therefore a pure mental process, as arithmetic is a mental process.

I do not therefore count for much the arguments based on the existence of beauty in the world; as, of course, I cannot admit that beauty has an absolute being, independent of beautiful things. Beauty, to me, must be cognisable by the eye, the ear, or some other organ of our sense; for beauty of thought is only a figure of speech, meaning that a thought is true or well-expressed; in a word, that it pleases us as certain harmonies of sense please.

Perhaps the most logical argument of the existence of God derived from the universe would be one drawn from analogy. It might be reasoned that as our bodies, and the bodies of other organic things, have a vital principle, therefore the universal body too has a vital principle, a mind. But it would be more consistent, according to this reasoning, to give to each of the stars its God. Such speculations are besides quite foreign to our present argument, which requires a personal God, the overseer and ruler of the world.

Of God's justice and mercy in the living universe we have not yet spoken, and I think I should prefer to leave it to you to point out instances of these, if you think the case requires it. I confess that, for my part, I see little in the general arrangements of nature to indicate either. Indeed, I have always considered it one of the strongest arguments in favour of a future life, to all who believe in a good God, that the injustices of the present world need redress. Like you, I do not complain of my individual lot. I have probably had my full share of pleasure in life; and if the future has, as it doubtless has, an increasing balance of pain in store for me, it is probably my due. But it would be difficult to maintain that all creatures are equally fortunate. I knew of one, a young lady who died at the age of thirty, and who, for the last five years of her life, suffered constant pain in the form of ear-ache, to the extent that her hair turned white, and that she eventually died of it. She was a good and pious person; and accepting this as a visitation from God, she prayed that this pain might cease before she died, if it was only for half an hour; but her relations assure me that to the last the pain continued, and that she had no conscious interval free from it till death took her. It seems difficult to understand, except on the supposition of a future life, how justice was here dealt. Still less is there a sign of mercy, such as we understand it; certainly not, as Balmes puts it, of mercy of a sentimental kind.

I have seen cattle, in the Pampas, caught in a kind of natural trap, contrived by the holding mud at the bottom of the water holes where they came to drink. Here they suffer the precise torment of Tantalus, the water gradually drying up out of their reach under a burning sun. At the end of a week they die. I do not say that nature is cruel, in spite of such instances as these, but that it is careless. There is a want of that feeling of pity which in ourselves is provoked by entreaty. Without being a sentimentalist, I think that, if a gnat had stung me, and it could beg for its life in such words as some have used in praying God to be released from it, I would open the window and let him go. It is easy to say, "God is good, therefore there is no real injustice in the world ; and, if He does not always hear our prayers, it is that we do not always know what is best for us." But for this we must start with a belief in Him. I would conclude this subject with a quotation from a great authority, which is more or less to the point, though the evils spoken of by him are not mere physical evils.

"I look out of myself into the world of men, and there I see a sight which fills me with unspeakable distress. The world seems simply to give the lie to that great truth" (the existence of God) "of which my whole being is so full; and the effect upon me is in consequence, as a matter of necessity, as confusing as if it denied that I am in existence myself. If I looked into a mirror and did not see my face, I should have the sort of feeling which actually comes upon me, when I look into this living busy world and see no reflexion of its Creator. This is to me one of the great difficulties of this absolute primary truth, to which I referred just now. Were it not for this voice speaking so clearly in my conscience and my heart, I should be an atheist, or a pantheist, or a polytheist, when I looked into the world." . . . "The sight of the world is nothing else than the prophet's scroll full of 'lamentations, and mourning, and woe.'"

"To consider the world in its length and breadth, its various history, the many races of men, their starts, their fortunes, their mutual alienation, their conflicts ; and then their ways, habits, governments, forms of worship ; their enterprises, their aimless courses, their random achievements and acquirements, the impotent conclusion of long standing facts, the tokens so faint and broken of a superintending design, the blind evolution of what turn out to be great powers or truths; the progress of things, as if from unreasoning elements, not towards final causes, the greatness and littleness of man, his far-reaching aims, his short duration, the curtain hung over his futurity, the disappointments of life, the defeat of good, the success of evil, physical pain, mental anguish, the prevalence and intensity of sin, the pervading idolatries, the corruptions, the dreary hopeless irreligion, that condition of the whole race, so fearfully yet exactly described in the Apostle's words, 'having no hope and without God in the world' —all this is a vision to dizzy and appal, and inflicts upon the mind the sense of a profound mystery, which is absolutely beyond human solution." *

And now I shall be doing no more than is called for of me, if I state in terms the alternative to which a rejection of God the Creator reduces me, and which is Matter as the self-existent being. I will therefore explain to you, in a few words, my view of materialism as a positive belief, and sketch its primary dogmas.

In the same way then that a deist ascribes attributes to God, the materialist ascribes all or most of these to his own necessary being, matter, only with this difference, that whereas the former is an *à-priori* conception, the latter has the pretension of being the result of experience.

Thus the materialist affirms that *Matter is Eternal*. The observations of chemistry, geology, astronomy, and the known history of the world, seem to shew that at no period has a single monad of matter been added to or taken away from the material universe; and there is nothing to shew that any process of decay is at

* Newman : *Apologia*.

work to suggest an end. Matter changes constantly in form but not in substance. The primal elements combine, are separated, and form new combinations; but no new element is brought into being, nor is anything lost. In the absence of any limiting power, of whose existence there is no evidence, matter then may be supposed eternal.

Again *Matter is infinite.* All the researches of astronomy fail to discover a limit to space, or of the luminous bodies which compose the heavens. Who shall venture to fix the number of the stars? Nor has the microscope yet shewn a limit to the divisibility, to the inward extension of matter, if I may so speak. Matter then, in the absence of a limiting power, would seem infinite.

But *Matter is all powerful.* In it reside all powers, all forces, even the force of mind. For mind itself is but a mode of its action. Matter may even be said to be *all just*, though with an unconscious justice, *all wise*, with an unconscious wisdom, *all beautiful*, though unconscious of its beauty. It is even *the Creator*, for it has created thought. Here are the very attributes which have been ascribed to God, all but the attribute of consciousness; and even that matter has at length evolved. Is the materialist then without reason, when he defines matter after God's own symbol, "I am that I am," *Matter is that which is?*

Thus stated, it is difficult to accept the validity of an argument for a prior cause. If the Deist asserts that mind created matter, the materialist with a far stronger array of evidence shews that matter has produced mind, not indeed out of nothing, but out of itself. At least he can point to the fact that matter is constantly found unconnected with mind, but never mind unconnected with matter. Is it then any refuge from the weakness of our mental conceptions to substitute an eternal mind for an eternal matter?

I cannot find it so. But enough of this, which I am afraid is just the talk with which you "find it difficult to keep patience." You must however try to do so, and to believe me,—Yours affectionately,

PROTEUS.

P.S.—You will not, I am sure, quarrel with me for having, even in matters connected with metaphysics, adhered to the common-sense argument so dear to Balmes. Bishop Berkeley's position with regard to matter I accept as an intellectual stalemate; but it could hardly further our purpose to consider it where the question of God's existence is at stake. For how shall we believe in God whom we have not seen, if we believe not in matter which we *have* seen?*

* It was not *matter*, properly so called, but *material substance* that Berkeley denied. But there is no experience of substance: it is a transcendental idea.—A.

LETTER VII.

AMADEUS TO PROTEUS.

A cryptograph decyphered. The "Riddle of the Universe." "It is IMPOSSIBLE *there should not be a God"! "What is Law?"*

MY DEAR PROTEUS,—Some years ago I saw the following mysterious characters inscribed on the fly leaf of the *Times* newspaper:

"Ur ikc wecri, frg wjcpp dfjc. Lfniv wenuaopuow, frg eujcw anuj Xfik. Wcrg ikc rccgaop. Inowi tw xnuhcr nccg : xcwtgcw ikc Ncfgv tw sfricg iu wsfddcn stikfp. Inopv. M."

Being half out of sorts, and half indolent, and taking it for granted that I had before me a cryptograph, I set myself to unriddle this riddle, instead of betaking to my usual serious pursuits. I had read Poe's ingenious story of the *Gold Beetle*, and that was all the cypher lore I had to help me. According to "mine author," the character most frequently repeated is the letter *e*, and that letter is the one most frequently doubled. Now the character most frequently repeated and doubled in the writing before me is the character *c*. It is repeated eighteen times and doubled twice. No other letter is repeated so often, and none doubled more than once. Then *c* of the cryptograph should be *e* of the alphabet. I now examine the word *nccg*, which occurs in the second line of the cypher.

Meet? feet? seem? seed? deed? need? feed? heed? jeer? feel? heel? are tried in vain. At last I remember the word *reed*, an unlikely word to be used, and most used in the Scripture phrase about "*bruising the broken reed.*" I counted the letters in the foregoing word, to see if they corresponded with the number of letters in the word *broken*. I was somewhat startled to find they did; (The word of the cypher was xnuhcr). Not only so, but here was the character *c* in the very place it was to be expected, standing for *e* (if I was right) in the last syllable of *broken*. Nevertheless, I did not get on with my solution for some time, and was proceeding with another fancied clue, when suddenly I stopped. Could the combination *xnuhcr nccg*, corresponding with the number of letters in the words "broken reed," and capped by the appropriate occurrence of the *c* in its proper place at the end of *broken*, be the work of chance? a mere coincidence? Most improbable. Why the chances would be a hundred to one, a thousand to one, a million to one against it! It was almost impossible—*practically* impossible,—that I had not made out the cypher. I persevered; and presently the cryptograph yielded up its secret. It was the correspondence of a thief, or swindler with his mate.*

Now let us consider the universe as such a riddle, or cypher. The figure should be congenial to the mind of Proteus; for more than once, he speaks of the "Riddle of the Universe." † After Paley and

---

* *On the scent, and smell game. Party scrofulous, and comes from Bath. Send the needful. Trust is broken reed; besides the Ready is wanted to swagger withal.* Truly J.

† "Songs and Sonnets:" by *Proteus*.

Balmes, you compare the universe to a watch; but, if that comparison hold good throughout, there ought to be no riddle in the matter. One can examine the watch completely, find how part corresponds with part, and discover the whole plan; but of the universe we can only know a section; and of that section you only give me a section to consider. The American Government presented the Japanese with a little steam ship. These ingenious people soon detected the plan of the engine, and before two years had expired, a similar contrivance of their own floated on the sea of Japan. Supposing they had only had a section of the engine put before them, and had been asked, out of that to construct the whole engine, it would have been a riddle.

I have no doubt that if, with the larger eyes of an angel, you could examine the universe, you would be not merely, "struck with the neatness and finish of the whole thing," but would read the Maker's Name intelligibly written, as on your watch. It seems I have a right to say so, if, in the section of the inorganic world which is given me to consider, I find, as I trust I shall, unmistakeable evidence that it is part of a plan, of a vast machine, which reveals a mind worthy of such a work, and which we feel we can only worthily think of as Infinite.

First, on observing the heavens with the eye of science, we lose that beauty which ravishes the unscientific gaze of childhood; and then comes the disappointment which you express so forcibly. What means all this? These huge globes poised in space, how do they reveal God more than the pebbles on the seashore, to which you have likened them? There is one of them, the nearest to our earth, and which therefore, with the aid of a good telescope, I can examine. I do so; and behold the Queen of Heaven, as we were accustomed to style her, bathed though she be in the sunlight—nothing more nor less, as far as I see, *but a huge cinder!* Science professes to explain to us the Book of Nature; and behold, to carry out the metaphor, the Book is written in a cypher, which seems as unmeaning at first sight as the characters which I have traced at the head of this letter!

Well : what I want to do first is to see if there be any trace of method in this infinite, huge maze. If there be, I shall know that I am confronted with a mind like our own. There is one thing which encourages me at the start. These *pebbles* scattered on the shore of Immensity are *round*, and, as you observe, they seem rounded by law ; moreover their orbits are round too, or else elliptical. Then we have regular figures to deal with in this cypher. Here seems to me a streak of light. Regularity means law ; and law—what is that? If the law mean only *an inherent property of the body itself*, then I get nothing from regularity ; but if law be a rule of the body, not inherent in the body, but communicated to it *ab extra*, then the regularity of the heavenly-bodies is very significant.

For, surely, we must reason about matters of Natural Theology as about any other practical matters. Suppose you found yourself in an island, and doubted whether or not it was inhabited; and you suddenly came upon a plot of ground, whereon certain vegetables were planted in squares, exactly a foot distance from one another, would not this regularity be assigned by you to design? Law then supposes intelligence, but this intelligence is not inherent in the bodies themselves; so you say yourself: "A stone," in being attracted towards the earth's centre, "acts blindly, unconsciously," and yet according to law—whose law? Not only is the intelligence not in the bodies themselves, it is not even in the laws themselves. "There cannot however," says the author of the *Vestiges of Creation*, "be an *inherent intelligence* in these laws. The intelligence appears external to the laws, something of which the laws are but as the expressions of the Will and Power."* "There is a mistake," says Paley (quoted by the same author)† "concerning the idea which the term law expresses in physics, whenever such a term is made to take the place of power, and as such, to be assigned for the cause of anything, or of any property of anything, that exists. A law pre-supposes an agent, for it is only the mode according to which an agent proceeds: it implies a power, for it is the order according to which that power acts. Without this agent, this power, which are both distinct from the law, the law is nothing, does nothing."

This statement concerning law, which might be confirmed by other authorities, signifies, if I rightly understand, that *bodies, in themselves, are not heavy;* and that the gravitation, which has rounded the planets and holds our system of worlds together, is the *hand of God!* I have used the word system too hastily, perhaps; for system supposes a plan; and you ask, "What sign of purpose is there in this multiplicity of globes, with their endless revolutions or their endless fixity?" This question is moderately put. You do not ask me to

* "Vestiges of Creation," p. 9, Eleventh Edition.
† *Ibid., Note* 1. Natural Law.

solve (though Proteus thinks it hard upon him that he cannot solve) the "Riddle of the Universe;" I am only to show a *sign of purpose* in this section of a section of it under examination. I am not to declare what the purpose is. That is fair; and I think that more could not reasonably be expected under the circumstances. It is enough for me if I can discover that the work is the work of a mind analogous to our own; if I can get on the track of a plan, though what the plan be, as a whole, I am not able to discover. I have only got so far with the cypher of the universe, that its characters are symmetrical. This is a hopeful sign. Now I want some clue, at this stage of my progress, such as the "broken reed," in which, contradicting a proverbial expression, I trusted, not in vain, in solving the thief's cryptograph. And I find such a clue in the respective distances of the planets.

"It has been found," says the Author of the *Vestiges of Creation*,[*] "that, if we place the following line of numbers and add 4 to each, we shall have a series denoting the respective distances of the planets from the sun."

+ 4 (to each)	0	3	6	12	24	48	96	192
	4	7	10	16	28	52	100	196
	Merc.	Ven.	Earth.	Mars.		Jup.	Sat.	Uran.

Here is a most symmetrical gradation, since the progression, in the first line of figures, is by duplication. Now, when this relativity of the distances was first discovered, there was wanting a planet between Jupiter and Mars; Neptune was also wanting. Point 28 being vacant, it would have been with me a crucial

[*] P. 7, Eleventh Edition.

test, whether this rhythm were accidental or designed, if there were or were not something at 28. I know that the strangest coincidences are found in this matter of numbers, but on the discovery of a group of planets there, at a mean distance from the sun, between Mars and Jupiter, I think I should have exclaimed, "It is *impossible* there should not be a God!" The word impossible is not scientific here. That only strictly speaking is impossible which is contradictory. It is *possible* that the rhythm may be the result of chance,— about as possible as if you should shake the letters of the alphabet together, and turning them out on the table should find that they constructed a stanza of poetry!

With regard to Neptune, I understand from a note to the new edition of the *Vestiges*, that enough is not yet known about this planet to calculate accurately. You will see that, according to the proportion, the distance of Neptune from Uranus should be represented by the number 388.

The distances of the planets bear also a mathematical relation to the times of their revolution round the sun. Thus *the squares of the times of revolutions are to each other in the same proportions as the cubes of the mean distances of any two planets.** There are other relations which tend to show that it is a *system* we are dealing with; and that is enough for my present purpose.

Now system is a sign of purpose. What is the purpose of the universe? I do not know, but can only conjecture from what I know of our own planet. It is a world, the purpose of which seems to be to

* See "Vestiges," p. 8.

afford a dwelling place for millions of creatures, and to afford them also the means of such happiness as their several natures render them capable of enjoying ; and it would seem that the universe is just a system of such worlds. But how this purpose is carried out, and what is the nature of the beings in other planets than our own, for whose benefit this order is established, I do not know. The great gulf of space between us forbids such knowledge. Our satellite would seem to be an old world at present lying fallow, or else a new one in course of development. The origin of the planets in our system, as you observe, is the same. The material comes from the sun ; but whence their laws, revolutions, beauty, proportions ? Could the sun of itself have projected them *mathematically?* Whence is Law ? Affectionately yours,

AMADEUS.

P.S.—I leave the subject of evolution for the next letter.—A.

LETTER VIII.

AMADEUS TO PROTEUS.

Amadeus declares that the doctrine of Evolution is neither inconsistent with design in Creation, nor at variance with Catholic doctrine. " The question of our Ancestry."

MY DEAR PROTEUS,—Unless you had anticipated me, I had begun this letter with a glowing panegyric on Darwin's theory. As it is, I can only add to what you have said that, until I read the "Origin of Species," I never considered Natural History as a science, for science, as such, looks to the Universal, whereas I could never see in Natural History anything more than interesting particulars. True, my readings on this head had not gone beyond such books as White's "Natural History of Selborne," and I did not then know of the theory of evolution.

It never occurred to me until I read your letter that evolution could be considered as antagonistic to design. It is not so to my mind. Ever since I read that pretty illustration of the globes of oil in the *Vestiges*, I have believed that our whole planetary system was projected from the sun. The illustration seemed to me an exception to the dictum, "An illustration is not an argument," for this one is an argument, and a very good one. If then the globes are projected, and yet rhythmically and not at random like the fragments of a bombshell, this very much enhances to my mind the wisdom and power of the Creator.

And so with the evolution of plants and animals; it enhances my conception of the Creator's wisdom and power, if such evolution be not a blind fortuitous progress, but rhythmical, harmonious, and beautiful. So says Mr Wallace, who shares with Darwin the glory of the invention of the theory of Natural Selection. "Why," he asks, "should we suppose the machine too complicated to have been designed by the Creator so complete that it would necessarily work out harmonious results? The theory of continual interference is a limitation of the Creator's power. It assumes that He could not work by pure law, in the organic as He has done in the inorganic world."* But more of this in my next letter.

As to the relation between Faith and Science, I can only say that they who are *afraid of science* must have *a very weak faith*. I have always been taught that the Book of Nature and the Holy Scriptures are equally the Word of God. And as to the Church; if the history of Galileo teaches one thing more plainly than another it is this that, when opinion of science has passed into the domain of *fact*, the Church will recognise it as such, and allow an obscure passage in the one Book to be interpreted by a clear statement in the other.

The theory of evolution asks me to believe, (1) that geological time is practically infinite, (2) that the several species of animals, etc., were not *immediately* created by God, but only *derivatively*. Without any

* Quoted by St. George Mivart, "Genesis of Species," xii., p. 315.

fear of jeopardizing my faith, I can give a cordial *Credo* to both these demands.

I was taught the theory which regards the *Six Days* of Moses as indeterminate periods, by some or other of my Catholic instructors, so early that I cannot remember when I first acquired it.

The tradition must have come into the Church from the Jews, for I find that Philo accounts it "a piece of clownish simplicity to think that the world was made in six days or in any fixed time."* Origen † argues against those who, "interpreting Scripture literally, say that six days were taken up in the creation of the world." St Athanasius considers that "the *Verbum ante omnia genitum* can be no creature, because no creature was created before another; but all were made at once, by one *fiat.*" ‡ (We shall meet this latter opinion again, and I trust see that it is not prejudicial to the theory of evolution.) As to St Augustine, with whose great name this theory has been chiefly connected. "St Augustine," says Father Ryder,§ "upholds this view with all the subtlety of his intellect, and the wealth of his imagination. He regards the Mosaic account as representing an order of nature from the simple to the complex, not an order of time; and again, as a leaf taken from an angelic record, in which time, properly speaking, has no place, but only the gradual development of angelic knowledge and worship." This writer furnishes me with the subsequent history of the theory, which is highly instructive.

* Lib. 1. Allog.   † Lib. 1. Cont. Cels.
‡ Cont. Arian. Orat. ch. xxi.
§ "Mosaic Cosmogony," not published.

Albertus Magnus, the master of St Thomas Aquinas, and St Thomas himself, borrowed it from St Augustine; but in his last work, the "Summa," the latter's liking for it had cooled down. For, whereas in his Commentary he had styled it "more reasonable and protecting the Scriptures from the derision of infidels," yet in the Summa he has no commendation of it, but merely allows it to be held; he is only careful "*ut neutri sententiæ prejudicetur.*" Cajetan and Canus were the last supporters of the theory for some time. And Petavius tells us that, in his day, it had got out of fashion. "Commune omnium consensu hodie repudiatur; patronum ferè habere desiit." * And unfashionable it continued until, in our own days, Cardinal Wiseman drew attention to its claims. Indeed unfashionable is too weak a word; it was *reprobated.* "Arriaga † goes so far as to say that, had it not been for St Augustine's name, his opinion would long ago have been condemned as nothing short of heretical." Then Father Ryder remarks that, "It is hard not to smile, in spite of the common danger, when we see the Jesuits of to-day intrenching themselves against the attacks of geology behind the battered walls of the position their predecessors had been bombarding so assiduously and so lately."

Nothing can be clearer from these testimonies than that the Church has never condemned the theory of "The Days" as indeterminate periods.

Now for the next point, that the several species of plants and animals were not *immediately* created by Almighty God. Mr St George Mivart, the latest

---

* De Opere Sex. Dier., 1. 5. Quoted by F. Ryder.
† Op. S. D. Disp., 28. cit. ditto.

exponent of Evolutionism, is a Catholic, and approaches the subject armed to the teeth with patristic and theological authorities in favour of his orthodoxy.* He cites St Augustine to the effect, that God created organic forms "by conferring on the material world the power to evolve them under suitable conditions;" and St Thomas Aquinas, who declares, "that in the first institution of Nature we do not look for miracles, but for the laws of Nature" (quidquid natura rerum habeat); and that the various kinds were created *only derivatively* (potentialiter tantum), etc. etc. Cornelius à Lapide is introduced as asserting, "that at least certain animals were not created *absolutely*, but only *derivatively*," (Non fuerunt creata formaliter sed potentialiter.) And he clenches the argument, adduced from this *catena* of authorities, with a smart saying from Roger Bacon, that "The saints never condemned many an opinion which the moderns think ought to be condemned."

But so long ago as 1860 a writer in the Rambler † (I suppose, Simpson) had pointed out how congenial to the Fathers of the Church was the doctrine of evolution, commended, as it seemed, by the strict letter of Scripture: "Law and regularity, not arbitrary intervention, was the patristic ideal of creation. With this notion they admitted without difficulty the most surprising origin of living creatures, provided it took place by *law*. They held that when God said : 'Let the waters produce,' 'Let the earth produce,' He conferred forces on the elements of earth and water, which enabled them naturally to produce the various species of organic

* "Genesis of Species." † Rambler, March 1860.

beings. This power, they thought, remains attached to the elements throughout all time." The same writer points out that neither is the "survival of the fittest" a novel doctrine. It was objected to Aristotle that, by fortuitous combinations, organisms have been produced and perpetuated, such as final causes, did they exist, would have produced. "For when the very same combinations happened to be produced which the law of final causes would have called into being, those combinations which proved to be advantageous to the organism were preserved; while those which were not advantageous perished, like the minotaurs and the Sphinxes of Empedocles."*

From the citations of the Fathers you will have learnt, with St. George Mivart, to distinguish two kinds of creation,—the one *absolute*, of which St. Augustine says: "*Deus simul omnia creavit;*" and the other *derivative*, or, as we should say, by evolution.

Now as to the question of "our ancestry," according to the theory of evolution. Fortified by his theological authorities, Mr Mivart makes bold to assert that man's *body* was *not* created in the primary and absolute sense of the word, but only derivatively, *i. e.*, by the operation of secondary law. His *soul*, on the other hand, was created in quite a different way, not by any pre-existing means external to God Himself, but by the direct action of the Almighty, symbolised by the term "*breathing*." "God made man from the dust of the earth, and breathed into his nostrils the breath of life." Again, he says, "That it is not necessary to suppose that any action, different in kind, took place in the production of man's body,

* Rambler, ad loc. citat.

from that which took place in the production of the bodies of other animals, and of the whole material universe." But how as to the production of the body of the woman? in which Holy Scripture seems to assign a plainly different origin to that of the bodies of other animals: "The Lord God cast a deep sleep upon Adam; and when he was fast asleep, He took one of his ribs . . . . and the Lord God built up the rib, which He took from Adam, into a woman."

But my scruple is not altogether a theological one. I cannot think that the first human pair had brute parents on other grounds, and am glad that so distinguished an authority as Mr Wallace claims a supernatural origin for "the human form divine." Natural selection he considers unequal to account for the brain, the hand, and the human voice, the distribution of the hair on the body, and the absence of the prehensile foot, "useful in climbing, and not incompatible with erect locomotion." Man, as to body, as well as soul, is thus exempted from the absolute control of selection.* Is he not worthy of

---

* It is only just to Mr Mivart to note here, that he too exempts the body of man from the exclusive action of the law of selection. Speaking of Mr Wallace's objections to the theory,—that man's body was created in a similar manner to that of other animals, *i. e.*, by selection, he says: "The validity of these objections is fully conceded by the author of this book; but he would push them much further, and contend (as has been now repeatedly said) that another law, or other laws, than "Natural Selection," have determined the evolution of all organic forms and inorganic also."—*Genesis of Species*, ch. xii. [Since the above went to press, a friend writes to me: "There is no difference between Mr Wallace's theory and that of Mr Mivart, concerning the formation of man's body. They both contend for the co-operation therein of artificial (Divine) selection; but Mr Mivart extends this to the rest of the material universe." I am glad to be corrected on the point.]—A.

such exemption? But, of course, that is a matter of facts and argument.

I have only considered hitherto the law of evolution in itself, and as concerned with theology. I have now to consider Darwin's exposition of it,—the theory of natural selection.

But this portion of my subject must be left for another letter, in which I trust to shew that the reason why that theory explains such a vast number of facts hitherto unexplained, is because the theory of evolution, on which it reposes, must be considered true; and that the reason why, notwithstanding, so many facts remain obstinately inexplicable by Darwin's theory, is because natural selection is not the *only* account of the origin of species.—

Affectionately yours, AMADEUS.

LETTER IX.

AMADEUS TO PROTEUS.

How Amadeus was affected on reading the "Origin of Species." Strong and weak points in the theory of Natural Selection. Three tests. The present stability of organic forms. Certain questions of Proteus answered.

MY DEAR PROTEUS,—I must begin this letter by stating that though, like yourself, I have always taken a lively interest in the works of nature, and have carefully read Darwin's *Origin of Species*, I am not a naturalist; and therefore must try to speak with becoming modesty on this portion of my subject.

Now I will tell you how I was affected on the first reading of Darwin. First of all, I was in raptures with the book; for, although I thought there must be some flaw in the theory, yet when I considered the numerous curious facts on which it threw a flood of light, and which would be otherwise unmeaning, I could not think it was matter to be condemned as wholly atheistic and abhorrent. Of course I believed that God created every *real* species; while varieties, I thought, might be wholly the work of circumstances through natural selection. But, even amongst really distinct species, the theory suggested a *mysterious connexion*, which, I argued, we ought not to ignore, because we did not understand the manner of it.

My clerical friends laughed, and said, "that I was *bitten.*"

As for the mysterious connection, I sought it in the *making* of the world, not in the *world as made*—*in fieri*, not *in facto esse.* Hence, I thought that one need not look for close intermediate links between the several species, either in the natural world, as it exists, or in the geological record. If, at that time, I had adverted to the distinction of the schoolmen between *absolute* and *derivative* creation, it would have expressed my meaning. In this sense, and as pronounced of the world *in fieri,* I held a theory of evolution—not dogmatically, but as a mere theory to satisfy my craving after scientific unity. I had been reading Dante's *Purgatorio,* and was arrested by Statius' discourse on Generation.* Here, I said, Nature betrays the secret of how she works; all forms from the lowest fungus to the highest mammal pass under the Divine finger in the moulding of man. In some sense or other, then, the theory of evolution was true.

Here is Darwin's strong point, it seems to me—the explanation of such a multitudinous array of facts, such as the rudimentary legs in serpents, teeth of beasts of prey in ruminants, stripes on horses, speckles on birds in their first plumage, similarities in the structure of distinct species, analogous structure of living and extinct species, etc., etc.†

Now let me say what I consider the weak points in Darwin's theory. Natural Selection does not explain the instinct of animals, nor, as you also have observed,

* Canto xxv. 37.
† What agent but Natural Selection can explain the hermit crab ?—A.

the beautiful in natural objects, and, while assuming that the varieties and species are not really distinct, it is met by the insuperable barrier of the infertility of hybrids. On the first and second of these topics I shall have some remarks to make presently. First, I wish to say a few words on Natural Selection itself.

Selection gives no real account of the origin of species, for it does not account for the individual ; and we must have the individual before the species. It accounts as to how the individual is *preserved*, but not as to how he is *produced*. You say, Given once the reproductive system, and like produces like with a difference ; but it is left unexplained why like should produce like, either with or without a difference : "The origin of even an individual animal or plant," says Mr Mivart, "what determines the embryo to evolve itself; *e.g.*, as a spider rather than a beetle, is shrouded in obscurity ; *à fortiori* must this be the case with the origin of species"* (Here let me observe that the reproductive system itself is characterised throughout nature by *contrivance;* so that the argument of design is, so far at least, uninterfered with by Natural Selection).

As with the individual so with the species. Selection shows how a race favoured with a certain organ will be conserved in the struggle for life, but I submit that selection does not account for the existence of such or such an organ.

For instance, you ask me if I can suggest anything as to the homologous structure of the upper and lower jaws.† Well, as I understand it, every embryo

* Genesis of Species, ch. 1, p. 1.
† Proteus asked this, *à propos* of the *mathematical* element in the organic world ; but I have treated on this aspect of the subject later on.—A.

of vertebrates commences with a longitudinal streak —that I suppose is the spinal cord. Now the vital activity contained therein will act with equal force on either side. Thus, at *a a* it produces arms, wings, or paddles; at *b b* legs or paddles; at *c c* the scull bones, wrapping round to meet and form the upper jaw; and at *d d* the jaw bones, wrapping round to form the corresponding lower jaw. This is a contrivance so suggestive that it arrested your attention at once; it enables the organism to eat and live. But I do not ask Darwin (for I know he cannot tell me without going out of his theory) why the vertebral column should germinate at *a* or *b* or *c*, rather than elsewhere. It may be said indeed that, if the member attained to the merest rudiment, it would get selected, if useful; just as, *e.g.*, the roughness in the cat's tongue becomes prickles in larger quadrupeds, and teeth on the tongue of a trout. Granted : I do not want to deny absolutely the agency of natural selection. A useful rudiment, then, would get selected; but it is the rudiment I want to account for. It seems to me that the structure of the skeleton of man or beast, but especially the formation of the bones of the skull, is only to be explained on the principle of contrivance; so that, once more, on the theory of evolution the argument from design maintains its ground.

My quarrel with natural selection is, that it is made *the sole* account of the origin of species. Certainly this principle must be of indefinite vastness of application. It explains one fact which nothing else explains, the existence in Australia, and nowhere else, of the fossils of marsupials, and the existence in America and nowhere else of the fossils of sloths and armadillas; showing that these species owe their existence, at least as an *occasional cause*,* to selection through circumstances indigenous to those respective countries:—I say, as an occasional cause; for when I try to make selection the sole account, whether of individual or species, I cannot even make a start. And yet philosophers of this school would ask me to explain, not merely the whole organic world, by this one law, but attributes for which the most venerable authority has always sought a higher source—the instinct of animals, the beautiful in nature, and even the moral attributes of man!

I now propose to try Darwin's theory by application to three species, for which, I think, it notably fails to account. And my first is the *Hunting Spider*, which I find located in Natural History, under the name of *Salticus Scenicus*. This spider, unlike most of its congeners, spins no web, though provided with the means of doing so, but roving at large, hunts its prey —the common house-fly, which it secures by leaping on him. Its colour, of mottled black and white, exactly imitates the surface of stuccoed walls of the Roman dwellings, on which I first observed him. And this imitation is very necessary; for the house-flies, out of doors, are very nimble and difficult to catch. The movements of the spider showed, in the

* By occasional cause I do not mean a cause that acts only occasionally, but a cause improperly so called, which is the occasion of the effect being produced, but not the *motive power* which produced it.—A.

plainest manner, that he appreciated his advantage; when he drew up his legs, and flattened himself to the wall, as a fly settled near him, it required a keen eye indeed to distinguish him from one of the many excrescences on the mottled wall. I never saw him jump on the back of his prey: he waited until the fly sprung up, when he sprung with him, attaching himself to the wall by a single thread; and seizing the fly, the two swung together, while the spider sucked his victim's blood.

Now, in a garden which I used to frequent, when in Rome, were several huge tree-pots, in which orange-trees were planted; and, on these pots, powdered with a fine green dust or mould, I found my friend, and lo! he was green, the colour of the pot! The mottled markings were on his body; but all was suffused with a greenish hue, to a shade the colour of the surface on which he sported. I last saw him on the post of my house-porch, a dim dusty hue, like the post itself, which has not been painted since the house was built. Now, to account for this creature, I want two factors—an inborn proclivity to vary the colour in conformity with the surrounding surface, and a saltatory power in the structure of the legs, (the common spider is no jumper.)

I think this is a special *crux* for the Darwinian hypothesis. Because, as certain individuals would be equal to the colouring proclivity while below the mark in saltatory power, and others *vice-versa*, the selection would be continually put at cross purposes with itself—and when I add to this, that the offspring, in each generation, though always having the tendency to vary, yet have such tendency to vary, not in one fixed direction, but in every direction; and when I consider further that the *practical infinitude of geological time* is out of place here, where walls and door-posts of yesterday are concerned, I think the chances of such a creature getting selected would be millions to one. Still I would admit its account even by selection, postulating a minute providence,[*] such as the doctrine of a supramundane Deity supposes; but this would be going out of the Darwinian hypothesis, in which the selection is blind, inexorable, fortuitous!

I select my next, as also my third instance, from St George Mivart's *Genesis of Species*.

How can selection alone account for the whale? The baleen, or whalebone, in this creature's mouth acts as a sieve, which, when the animal swallows a gulp of water, retains the minute marine creatures on which it feeds : of what use would be the *rudiment of a sieve?* How then did the whale get selected?

In spite of the marsupials furnishing a strong point in favour of natural selection, I think Mivart has shown, in the instance of the kangaroo, that selection can by no means be the sole agent here. Thus, it appears that the young kangaroo is born so utterly helpless that it cannot suck; and, meanwhile, its nutrition is contrived as follows :—The mother is gifted with a muscular development of the mammary gland, by means of which she injects the milk into the throat of her young; but such injection would be attended with suffocation, were it not met with a reciprocal arrangement on the part of the offspring, which has the larynx elongated, so as to meet the lower end of the

[*] By providence I do not mean any interference with the laws of nature; providence is *provision*.—A.

nasal air-passage; and the creature breathes through the tubal larynx, while the milk finds its way into the gullet; and the suffocation is thus avoided. As to this reciprocal contrivance, Mr Mivart asks, "How did the elongated larynx itself arise, seeing that, if its development lagged behind the maternal structure, the young primeval kangaroo must have been choked; while without the injecting power in the mother it must have starved?" And he remarks ironically that the "struggle for life must have been *severe indeed* in this case!" The argument from design doubles itself, let me here say, where these reciprocal relations are concerned. If selection is to account for them it cannot be the blind fortuitous selection of Darwin.

Before I take leave of this portion of my subject, I must regret that I am not a naturalist, and must content myself with the ungracious task of destroying, instead of building up, a theory of evolution. Mr Mivart's conclusion, that *natural selection acts as subordinate agent to some higher law or laws unknown*, is far too meagre and negative for ambitious spirits like yours and mine, which would fain unriddle this riddle of the universe; but, at least, let us be patient under our ignorance. Nature is a beneficent mother, and no sphinx to devour us if we cannot answer her *how* and *why?* As to my theory of development *in fieri* and not *in facto esse*, it was a mere dream of the imagination; as I could not bring it into contact with facts geological, which might soon convict it of utter absurdity. Still it is curiously suggestive that Nature works up to the higher through the lower grades in the production of an organism—suggestive, as I said in the beginning, that in some sense or other *the theory of development must be true*.

The ardent disciple of Darwin, who has looked at the organic world through his master's spectacles, when he shuts up his book, and turns to look at the world as it is, must be startled at the contrast. Not, in the actual, not in the geological world, as Darwin frankly confesses, will he find those " infinitely numerous fine transitional forms," which ought, on the theory, to link the different species together. How stubborn, obstinate and fixed, on the whole, are the world, and its inhabitants ! Hence, no wonder that, as Darwin admits, the authority of naturalists is against him :—
" The most eminent palæontologists, Cuvier, Agassiz, Barande, Pictet, Falconer, Forbes, etc.; and all our greatest geologists, Lyell, Murchison, Sedgwick, etc., have unanimously, often vehemently, maintained the *immutability of species !* I feel how rash it is to differ from these authorities, to whom, with others, we owe all our knowledge."* Certain forms—sheep, cattle, dogs, pigeons are flexible enough—*to a certain extent*. Here, one would think, there was opportunity to put the theory to a practical test ; for the variable potency does not require the ages of geological time to operate in; it is excessively rapid. Let then the cunning sheep-breeder, who "seems as if he had chalked out upon a wall a form perfect in itself, and then had given it existence," or the pigeon-fancier who will produce you "any given feather in three years," (but it would take him six years to obtain head or beak) let them produce two breeds, so opposite as to be barren, either in themselves or in their offspring, and the thing is done.

* "Origin of Species," chap. ix.

On the other hand, there are, it seems inflexible organisms—what more stable than a goose? The goose, says Darwin, seems to have a "singularly inflexible organism"—an unfortunate admission, which, as Mivart remarks, practically gives up the question. Why, if Darwin's theory be absolutely admitted, animal nature is of *its very essence flexible*. Then, there is the insuperable barrier to indefinite variability imposed by the infertility of hybrids. Explain this fact as we may, it is a fact, and, if nature works by design, it has a purpose. It is strange, on Darwin's theory, that canaries should not be perfectly fruitful with their congeners the linnets and other *fringillidæ* in this country.

Nature then, I venture to say, is *fixed*. It is not indefinitely developing, but *it has developed*. "There are reasons for thinking," says Mivart, "that the human race is a witness of an exceptionally stable and unchanging condition of things," which Mr Croll and Mr Wallace attribute to climatical causes. However it be accounted for, such is the acknowledged fact. Some forms have become extinct, almost in our own days—as the dodo; but no new species, at least of the higher types of organized life, as far as I can discover, has been registered. *We are living in the seventh day, the sabbath of God's rest.*

The programme, which I propose to myself, in dealing with the matters suggested in your letters, is as follows:—(1) the instincts of animals, (2) the beautiful, in nature and art (3) the moral attributes of God, (4) immortality.

But, before entering on these subjects, I must endeavour, if only I can succeed, to satisfy you on these points as to which you question me: Can I suggest anything, (1) as to *mathematical proportions in nature?* (2) Can I furnish an instance "of a natural organ, which presents the features of a reasoned choice of means?" (3) Is there anything in nature analogous to pictorial imitation?

1. "In the organic world, the mathematical element," you observe, "is conspicuous by its absence." Surely this is too broadly stated, and I shall venture to qualify it; indeed you have qualified it yourself. By the mathematical element, I take it you mean rhythm, balance, proportion, and regularity of figure. It is true I think, that, except where purpose is concerned, nature nauseates absolute regularity; a fact which I shall have to consider in dealing with the beautiful. Where purpose is concerned, *i.e.* where it is absolutely needed, there is regularity enough.

The double members of the body, the correspondence in the number of the teeth, toes, and fingers, are instances which you suggest. I find that there was a species of deer, in which, by some freak of nature, the antler only branched on one side of the head; but it was abolished, I suppose, by natural selection. This doubling of members is repeated throughout the whole organic world. I can account, as I have said, by natural selection for its *preservation;* but for its *origin* I want *purpose.* The vital activity acting equally on both sides of the trunk of a tree, why should not the branches, stems, leaves, correspond in position, number, and proportion, as the members of animals, but that no useful purpose would be gained by an exact correspondence in these matters, and by a surfeit of regularity the beautiful would be depressed? Where purpose is concerned, the regularity seems even superfluous to the occasion, as in the workmanship of the birds and insects. What can be more mathematical than the hexagonal cells of the honeycomb; or what more regular than the eggs and nests of the smaller birds? and I trust to shew, in its proper place, that this is really God's work. Nor do I see the absolute need of that very mathematical symmetry, and absolute finish and polish of the habitations of certain shell-fish.

2. As an instance of an organ which presents the features of a reasoned choice of means, take the structure of the jaws with their teeth, above alluded to, which seems to me as good an instance of adaptive design, as the vice with its teeth in a blacksmith's shop; the only difference being,—that the vice is adapted to hold fast, not to masticate; and therefore, its jaws want the sidelong, semi-rotatory movement, which is necessary for mastication.

Then, as instances of exceedingly complex contrivance, take the following processes, by which fertilisation is effected in orchids, quoted from Darwin's *Origin of Species*:—" In one *(Coryanthes)*, the orchid has its lower lip enlarged into a bucket, above which stand two water-secreting horns. These latter replenish the bucket; from which, when half-filled, the water overflows by a spout on one side. Bees visiting the flower, fall into the bucket and crawl out by the spout. By the peculiar arrangement of the parts of the flower, the first bee which does so carries away the pollen mass glued to his back; and then, when he has his next involuntary bath in another flower, as he crawls out the pollen mass attached to him comes in contact with the stigma of that second flower, and fertilises it." In the other example *(Catasetum)*, when a bee gnaws a certain part of the flower, he inevitably touches a long delicate projection, which Mr Darwin calls the antenna. "This antenna transmits a vibration to a membrane, which is instantly ruptured, this sets free a spring by which the pollen mass is shot forth like an arrow, in the right direction, and adheres by its viscid extremity to the back of the bee!"*

3. Is there anything in nature analogous to pictorial imitation? like the pattern of a skull on the death's-head moth? or, I add, like the clown's face on the back of the hunting spider? Here we come back to the drolleries of Nature, mimicking. I do not wish to attach too much importance to them. But I will observe that, if the likeness be not merely fanciful, like the weasels and camels in the summer clouds, or the giants and castles in the embers of the fire-grate, where the resemblance is only perceived by the dreamy gazer himself; if it have plainly a foundation in fact, so that the likeness occurs to several persons independently, and if nature works by design, and not *merely*

* Quoted by St. George Mivart from the 5th edition of the "Origin of Species," p. 236. The earlier editions do not contain these examples.

If, as an example of a reasoned choice of means, I have not alluded to the obvious instance of the structure of the eye, it is because Darwin considers that natural selection is equal to account for it [ch. vi.]; and so (on the principle which I have adopted throughout the controversy, of conceding, though, of course, merely for argument's sake, as much as possible,) I have preferred to cite instances, as to which he himself, as is apparent from his language, is staggered by the extravagant demands of his theory.—A.

by selection, then the likeness is designed.* What do the orchids gain in the struggle of life by their likeness to bees, flies, and spiders? Bees do not visit the bee-orchis to fertilise it; it is ingeniously adapted for self-fertilization; nor are flies, or spiders, partial to the other kinds. The advantage of the butterfly, which, when alighted resembles a leaf, and of other mimicking insects, is, as you say obvious, but I can hardly think it due to selection; while, that selection accounts for the creature that imitates, not only a stick, but the corrugation on the stick's bark, and the spotted fungus marks thereupon, is too much for my imagination. Here, on a small scale, is pictorial imitation. Is it enough?

All this imitation is to my mind very suggestive; and, if there be not much more of it than there is, I can understand that God can scarcely care much to imitate the patterns of men (which I think is what Proteus would like) such as the ball-and-socket ornament on the peacock's tail, which, however is very remarkable, considering the *shading* by which the

---

* The "pictorial imitations," and "drolleries" scattered over creation seem to me things with which, their ulterior purposes not being fully known, the Fancy is apt to deal as well as the Reason; things that rather remind us vividly of Design, than illustrate the higher workings of a Divine Design. They exhibit the quaintly pleasant ways of that "Nature" which the human mind loves to impersonate, that it may deal familiarly with great things, while also clearly affirming that Nature's office is ever vicarious and subordinate. The Materialist asserts his "Madre Natura" as a substitute for God. To the believer she is one who sits amid the Creation of the "Pater Deus," governing its material details through the rules prescribed to her. The lower servants of the household, and the children, sometimes think she is all in all. The grown up neighbours know her for Head Servant, and Nurse.—*Editor*.

effect is produced. Instead of God imitating the patterns of men, it is man who is learning to appreciate the patterns of God. Do you not see that the old conventional flowers are beginning to disappear from your dessert-service, and that graceful ferns, and life-like pansies and daisies are taking the place of the insipid regularities of the willow-pattern plate?

What would Proteus have, that God should woo him by stooping to copy the picture of a picture? that he should see the ineffable Name, יהוה flame, in golden characters, on the wings of the magnificent Bird of Paradise? God has not given reason to man that He should have to treat him thus like a child. His evidences are evident enough if they are such to that reason. For my part, I thank God that I find enough in the natural world to teach me to know Him and to love Him, which is my happiness. I ask no sign to the eye of the body, so long as my mental vision is clear.

The other matters must be postponed. I have already exceeded the limits of an ordinary letter. Vale.—Affectionately yours, AMADEUS.

P.S.—You ask if I can give an example, not only of reasoned choice of means, but of choice of material. If I understand the drift of the question, I doubt whether natural selection could account for the excretion of the enamel of the teeth, and wax of the ear, and nails at the finger tips; there are also certain seeds which excrete an enamel protective of the kernel, *e.g.*, the seeds which Italians call *lagrime di Giobbe* (Job's tears). There is a plant also in this country, but I do not know it, the seeds of which have the same property, if it be not really the same plant, Corn-gromwell (*lithospermum arvense*). Of course these features are obviously useful, and therefore would be preserved by selection if once they *began*. I would suggest also the membraneous wing of the bat, unless you think selection might be equal to the account of it.—A.

LETTER X.

AMADEUS TO PROTEUS.

Amadeus proves the existence of God from the instincts of animals, and shows the insufficiency of Natural Selection to account for them.

MY DEAR PROTEUS,—The old fashioned argument for the existence of a Supreme Being deduced from the mysterious instincts of animals is thus stated by Addison :

"There is not, in my opinion, anything more mysterious in nature than this instinct of animals, which thus rises above reason, and falls infinitely short of it. It cannot be accounted for by any properties in matter, and at the same time, works after so odd a manner, that one cannot think it the faculty of an intellectual being. For my own part, I look upon it as upon the principle of gravitation in bodies, which is not to be explained by any known qualities inherent in the bodies themselves, nor from any laws of mechanism, but, according to the best notions of the greatest philosophers, is an immediate impression from the *First Mover*, and the divine energy acting in the creatures." "Spectator," Vol. ii. No 120.

In this statement of the case, I would venture to alter one particular. The instinct of animals does not *ever fall below* reason, but creatures endowed with it often in their actions fall infinitely below those endowed with reason, as they often rise vastly above them; where they fall below is in those cases in which, their instinct not aiding them, they are left to their own feeble intelligence. As Addison himself says, "Take a brute out of his instinct, and you find him wholly deprived of understanding." But again this statement wants qualifying. I have had a good deal to do with animals of one sort or another, and I by no means am disposed to underrate their intelligence; but certainly in the lower forms, it seems very feeble, while in the higher it is sometimes almost a match for reason itself.

I therefore distinguish, as every one who thinks carefully and observes must do, between instinct and intelligence, though popularly they are usually confounded. I do not admire the instinct of the elephant, or the dog, or the horse, or the parrot, or even the canary; for they are very intelligent indeed, and have less need of instinct, and consequently have, as far as I see, a meagre (comparatively speaking) share of it. On the other hand the hen, who by her instinct recognizes an enemy in the wheeling kite, does seem, in the words of Addison "a very idiot," when she mistakes a piece of chalk for an egg, is insensible of the increase or diminution in the number of those she lays, does not distinguish between her own and those of another species, and, at the appearance of ever so different a bird, will cherish it as her own.

If I descend to consider the insect world, I am surprised at their stupidity. The blue-bottle, which has blundered into my room, will spend hours in fruitlessly banging its head against the window pane, and if, at last, (as a dog or a cat would have done at first) it finds escape through the open door by which it entered, that is a mere accident : it blunders out as it blundered in. If, even from the ant, I am instructed to learn a lesson of wisdom, I do not think that she excels in this respect by superior intelligence,* but by the instinct which has raised her into a commonwealth ; for, when I have put very simple obstacles in her path I have found her utterly helpless in her embarrassment. The most familiar instance of the feebleness of intelligence in the insect world is a matter of common observation, as furnished by the gnat, which having once singed its wings in the candle, will raise itself on its half-shrivelled legs, and make again, in blind obedience to its instinct, for the fatal light. How different with the higher grades of animals ! I have been startled by the human behaviour of the elephant, who pats me on the shoulder with his trunk to attract attention, and then mimics the action of putting food into his mouth—behaviour more eloquent than speech ! Again, a friend of mine had a collie pup, for which when he cracked a bone with a hammer, the collie ran into the garden to fetch another bone which he had buried, in order that he might crack it in like manner ! but I can believe almost anything of the intelligence of a dog. I should weary you were I to proceed with the instances of intelligence of canaries and wild finches that I have tamed, and of the young of the wild rabbit, which Darwin considers almost untameable ; yet I cannot get into my subject without some allusion to these matters, and I shall even have to return to them when I consider the question of Immortality.

* See Postscript *a*.

When, then, I consider the undoubtedly highly gifted intelligence of the higher animals, I am amazed that the Cartesians should have explained all the phenomena of mental action in the brutes by blind instinct—I say *blind*, because it hardly requires proof that the white butterfly (to take Darwin's instance) does not know *why* she lays her eggs on a cabbage leaf. As to others, who, confounding reason with instinct, take the opposite course, of exaggerating the intelligence of the animals, and say it is only our pride which denies them the use of reason, the answer is obvious, that reason itself would be insufficient to preserve the life, for instance, of a swallow; and the hen, in like manner, wants a gift above reason indeed, to know (if she did know), before all experience, that a winged fowl will come out of the egg she sits upon.

Instead of this confusion between instinct and intelligence, I am persuaded that these endowments are in sharp contrast with one another. And, in the taming of the wild rabbit I just mentioned, I often said to myself, that the whole battle consisted in cultivating his intellect at the expense of his instinct. The battle succeeded so far, that when I gave him his liberty, he would not go away, but lingered about the grounds until he was devoured by a cat. I should even say then, that intelligence and instinct are in an *inverse ratio* (though I am not prepared to prove it) and that the one is at its *maximum* where the other is at its *minimum*. In man, where intellect is at its maximum, besides the stimulus of the appetites, I can hardly think of any instincts, unless they be the involuntary winking of our eyes, or the start at a surprise. If there be any truth in *presentiments*, I suppose this matter should be referred to instinct. These are *simple* instincts; in the lower orders of brutes we rise to contemplate most complex effects, as in the construction of the nests of birds, and the curious commonwealths of the bee and the ant.

Now, as to the origin of these wonderful instincts: The cultivated heathen sought it in God—

> " Equidem credo quia sit divinitus illis
> Ingenium."
>
> VIRGIL: *Georg.* i. 451.

God is as a reason to them which have none of their own. This seems to me the most simple account of the matter. And I think you will agree with me, that, if Darwin's attempt at explaining away the wonders of instinct is unequal to that effect; if it only starts difficulties instead of laying them; if it demands more credulity in us than simply to accept the Divine account; the argument for the existence of God shall stand.

There are three arguments against the theistical view of the matter; but none of them would avail to the denial that it is God who works here, in the teeth of the strong positive arguments that He does so work. They are :—

1. The loss of instincts (*e.g.*, under domestication); 2. The failure of instincts; 3. The odiousness of certain instincts.

Of the loss of instincts we have manifold experience; for the domestic rabbit will eat vegetables that are noxious, or even fatal to it; a parrot, escaped from its cage, cannot guide itself safely in its flight, but will dash itself against the boughs of the trees, until, as I have witnessed myself, it will fall trembling to the ground, and gladly suffer itself to be led back to its confinement. But this argument may easily be twisted the other way, and God be supposed to withdraw a light which is hardly needed when wild creatures are entrusted to the care of man; or, in the process of taming, the instincts are disused as the confidence in man increases; or the instinct may still speak, though unheeded; as an alarum ceases to wake the sluggard who habitually refuses to rouse himself at its call.

2. The failure of instincts is a more difficult matter. As an instance: a chaffinch stuck its nest against the rough bark of a tree. The fibres of moss, ling, and hair conglutinated with the bird's saliva, held sufficiently for a time; but the weight of five eggs, and the additional burden of the female's body at incubation time, were too much, and the nest began to decline from the perpendicular, and would have come away altogether, had not an intelligent boy come to the rescue, and banded the nest to the tree with strips of an old handkerchief, tacked with nails on either side. It was a comical sight to see the bird sitting on her eggs under these singular circumstances!

Again, an artificial duck-pond had been made, the basin being lined with clay mixed with sand. Now, the swallows, using the material thus unsuitably tempered to construct their nests, on the first heavy fall of rain, the whole of them were washed down. One bird, as if aware that the material was imperfect, unwove a piece of cord, and worked the hemp into the sandy clay. But in vain. Her nest came away with the others, and her eggs were broken. These failures argue nothing, you will observe, against the contrivance, *as a contrivance*, but only show the contrivance as unsuccessful in these instances. It is not that the instinct itself here fails; but the materials are insufficient for the purpose of the instinct. And if instinct guides the bird in the use of the material, as it does, yet, on the other hand, the bird can only avail itself of the best materials that come to hand. In the instance of the chaffinch, if she could have found a suitable *fork*, her instinct would have guided her to select it for a support for her nest; in its absence, she did the best she could.

3. As to the odiousness of an instinct, two chief instances are alleged by Darwin; the first being the case of the cuckoo, the rearing of which involves the destruction of certain tits or sparrows. Here I am confronted with the waste of life, and apparent carelessness of nature. But I hope to deal with this matter very soon, and I trust satisfactorily, in my letter on Immortality, and I will adduce considerations which, if they weigh equally with you as with me, will effectually banish the sting of death from the mere animal as from the human world. And, in the same letter, I shall deal with the subject of *pain;* so I omit now to consider Darwin's instances of instincts which cost pain to others. But the slave-making instinct in certain ants is very odious to Darwin. If however, the little slaves have kind masters, and the masters willing and affectionate slaves, (and this, from Darwin's most interesting account of them, seems to be the case), I think this sentimentalism out of place. But is this author's own system less ruthless? "Forward!" was Napoleon's only answer when told that a

G

regiment could not bear the fire of the enemies' guns; and "Forward" is still Darwin's word, in the system under consideration, "Forward" at all costs! "The general law, leading to the advancement of all organic beings" is "Multiply, vary, *let the strongest live, and the weakest die.*" There is a difficulty here, which I shall have to look straight in the face; but if there be a God, He is surely the author of the system in which this cruelty and waste, if there be cruelty and waste, is involved: what does Darwin gain by putting the difficulty back to the first link of the chain?

Now to consider Darwin's account of instinct. With its origin he has, he says, simply nothing to do. "I have nothing to do with the origin of the primary mental powers, any more than I have with that of life itself." Granted the beginning then, we go on smoothly in the old style. Instincts are as important as corporal structure for the welfare of the species, under its present condition of life; it is possible that slight modifications of instinct might be beneficial under changed conditions of life; it is possible, again, if instincts vary ever so little, (and they do vary) that natural selection may preserve and accumulate variations of instinct to any profitable extent. But "no complex instinct can possibly be produced through natural selection, except by slow and gradual accumulation of numerous, slight, yet profitable variations."[*] On this theory the highest flights of instinct, the hexagonal cells of bees, and the economical instincts of both bee and ant will get explained, and I shall lose a capital argument for the existence of God. But what are the facts adduced in support of these

[*] "Origin of Species," ch. vii.

slight, minute, gradual variations which the theory requires? Darwin says, that he is surprised to find "how very generally gradations leading to the most complex instincts can be discovered." However he only furnishes us with very few of them, and these not important, certainly inconclusive. Some ostriches lay their eggs in other birds' nests *of the same species*, or let them lie carelessly about; other smaller birds, besides cuckoos, do the same; certain bees are parasitic, and always lay their eggs in the nests of other birds— approaches to the instinct of the cuckoo, in the last case a similar instinct. Then, a pure terrier has been known to point like a pointer. Birds, again, agglutinate the hairs and fibres of their nests with saliva; the swallow tempers the mud of its nest with the same —approaches to the instinct of the N. American swift, which makes a nest exclusively of spissated saliva. Then, between the humble bee, which uses its old cocoons to hold honey, and adds separate, irregularly rounded cells of wax, for the same purpose, and the hive-bee which makes a double row of regular hexagonal cells, we have the Mexican Melipona, which constructs a nearly regular comb of wax, of which the cells are so close together, that they would intersect if the spheres were completed; but the bees do not allow this, and build flat walls at the points of intersection. So that, if Melipona made its spheres equiform and equidistant, we should have the hexagonal cell of the hive bee, as has been mathematically demonstrated.

These, I believe, are all the facts alleged; and they merely prove, to my thinking, that animals, especially of the same species, have oftentimes similar, or nearly similar instincts; what they certainly do not prove is, that natural selection is the *sole* account of instinct.

When, on the other hand, I consider the countless variety of curious and grotesque instincts, oftentimes exhibited within the same species, I see that *Natura non facit saltum* is a canon not applicable to the matter in hand; and that minute gradual variations are no more a way to explain the facts of the case than sliding up to it is a way to clear a five barred gate. The naiad-spider constructs a silken diving-bell; the mason-spider makes a practicable trap-door at the entrance of its subterranean abode. The weaver-bird plaits together the rushes of its nest; the tailor-bird stitches leaves together in definite seams, the ends being carefully tagged off and secured. The Cape gross-beaks club together into a commonwealth, and build a nest which requires a waggon and horses to carry it away. The Australian Megapodius makes an immense mound of vegetable matter, covered with earth, as her nest, in which she securely leaves her eggs to be hatched by process of fermentation. The commoner sorts of caterpillar swing a hammock, wherein to undergo their transformation; but the death's-head species buries itself in the ground for the same purpose. Some of the coleoptera sham death to escape their enemies, and will rather suffer themselves to be burnt than betray the counterfeit; others carry confusion into their adversaries' ranks by a series of explosions; again the larvæ of some cover themselves with fetid ejections, that of others with a mask of dirt and cobwebs, to disgust their insect-feeding enemies, etc., etc.

To meet the facts of the case, it is required, I

should say, that when a creature varies its instinct, it should *vary with a bound!* as in one instance, to which my notice was called, wherein a chaffinch in order to secure its nest to a tree wherein the fork was too taper for affording a rest, actually wove into the rim of the nest nearest to the fork a transverse sprig, more than a foot in length, which passed outside the fork, while the nest itself was thus slung by it securely on the other side. As I would hardly credit many a human being with so much thought, I cannot attribute this variation to the intelligence of the bird itself, but must account for it by the Author of its instinct. Besides the fact of the contrivance, it is not easy to see how the birds put it in execution.

The difficulties of selection seem altogether insurmountable in the case of the bee or the ant, where it is required that the instincts of a vast number should be simultaneously and (in the instance of individuals of different corporeal structure and habits) correspondingly modified. But the very formulation of the theory of variation, by instinct, is something very like a paradox. The various instincts *are acquired by certain trying circumstances in which, without such instinct, the creature could not subsist.* However, certain statements are paradoxical on paper, which in practice work smoothly enough; so let us consider the matter, not in the abstract, but go to the case of the cells of the bee.

The problem which the bees have practically to solve is this. How to produce a comb capable of holding the *maximum* of honey, while expending in its construction the *minimum* of wax? In order to effect this, I think the theory must postulate an indefinite series of successive, or nearly successive summers, so cold as just to thin off those bees which in their mode of working approximate least to the hexagonal cell, but not so cold as to threaten the extermination of the race. I say successive, or nearly successive cold summers; because, as instincts on this theory are essentially variable, on a remission of the severity of the weather, the circular tendency, still strong in inheritance, would be in danger of predominating. On this hypothesis alone, I think, can this circle become angular; but it is improbable to the very verge of impossible; and it is, surely, far easier to believe in a God who has gifted the hive-bee with this wonderful instinct.

The case of the ants brings in a startling difficulty. Some of the neuters differ widely both in size and structure, not only from their fertile brethren, but from one another; how then, did these get selected, since the principle of inheritance in the case of sterile neuters is eliminated? But the theory is equal to the occasion. Selection may be applied to the family, as well as to the individual. An ox is produced of the type required; the ox goes to the slaughter-house, but the breeder recurs with confidence to the *same stock*. So in this case, since sterile workers are required, why should not certain ants be gradually modified in instinct and structure, so as to produce such sterile workers? I cannot say why not, except that I suppose it must have *gone hard* with the family (gone hard in proportion to the utility of the workers) until the instinct and corresponding structure was perfected for producing these abnormal neuters ; and so the old see-saw returns, of the circumstances which require the instinct, which cannot do without the circumstances.

Darwin cannot forbear expressing his own astonishment at this feat of his theory, which here surpasses itself. "I should never have anticipated," he writes, "that natural selection could have been efficient in so high a degree, had not the case of these neuter insects convinced me of the fact." Fact!! why, it's all mere hypothesis! What shadow of proof is there, except that Darwin's theory requires it? But why should the theory require it in this case? This is a case, not of corporeal structure, but of instinct. What analogy is there between corporeal structure and mental endowments, that we should argue that the account of the one is the account of the other?

Darwin cannot disguise from himself, that his theory of instincts wants the support of facts. "I do not pretend," he says, "that the facts given in this chapter strengthen in any great degree my theory, *but none of the cases of difficulty to the best of my judgment, annihilate it.*" (*!!!*)

Darwin's theory, so usually luminous in explaining facts, is here conspicuously deficient. A few isolated examples are given, and they are all equally capable of being explained by design, on the old belief of a specially endowed instinct. "We can understand on the principle of inheritance, how it is that the thrush of South America lines its nest with mud, in the same peculiar manner as does our British thrush ; how it is that the hornbills of Africa and India have the same extraordinary instinct of plastering up and imprisoning the females in a hole of a tree, with only a small hole left in the plaster, through which the males feed them and their young when hatched ; how it is that the male wrens of North America build cock-nests to roost in, like the males of our distinct kitty-wrens." It has been suggested by writers who had no theory to contend for, that the material of the lining of the thrush's nest is designed for the sake of coolness; that wool and hair would be too heating for the bodies of the young. As to the imprisonment of female hornbills; it is obvious that the same maternal remissness of the females would be likely to be met in the same manner both in Africa and India, by an especially endowed instinct on the part of the males, particularly in the case of the same species. I suggest, in the instance of the cock-roosting nests, that it arises from the peculiar plan of the wren's nest, in which the design of concealment is not in the nest itself, *but only in the entrance to it.* The male sits in this cock's nest as sentinel, while the female incubates. In the case of a Cape tit-mouse (a case analogous) when the pair both leave the nest together, the male previously to leaving his sentinel box, "beats the opening of the nest violently with his wing, and succeeds in closing it, in order to protect his young from enemies." Thus design explains the cock-nests.*

As you ask, "Why are beautiful flowers?" so I ask, "Why do the birds sing instinctively,† each one its own little, unvaried strain?" For the purpose of getting *selected?* How is it then, that the celibate sings in his cage? By inheritance? But the rule with regard to structures, is, that when an organ is to no purpose, it becomes weak, unused, and ultimately aborted; and why, if Darwin's theory is to be applied to instincts, should not the same law apply to the song of birds? But, on the contrary, the canary's song is im-

* "The Universe," Pouchet.   † See Postscript.

proved by having been kept, time out of mind, in cages, and having its mating arranged for it. Its song, you will say, is improved by the selection of man. Yes; *the quality of note*; but this supposes the bird to sing; and indeed, the bird that won't sing cannot be made to sing. What can be clearer, than that a bird sings because he is happy,—when the sun shines out, when the morning breaks, when the gas is lighted? I do not see how selection could account for the song of birds; and I know of no *proof* that it does so account. I conclude on the whole with the following trilemma: Either instinct is nothing else than intelligence, which no scientific observer believes, or it is owing to natural selection, or there is a God, who is the Author of it.—Affectionately yours,   AMADEUS.

POSTSCRIPT.—*a. The Stupidity of Ants.* Mr Holt ("Science Gossip," July, 1868) says, "That the ants observed by him, seemed to have but very little idea of locality; and that, in their eagerness to obtain water, they fell into a tank in such numbers, as to threaten the extinction of the population; which can scarcely be considered an instance of sagacity." Mr Frederic Ward, according to the same journal, "Did not think that the ants observed by him got on in a workmanlike manner. He frequently noticed an ant come out with a piece of dirt in its forceps, and run about, apparently in a state of distraction, as if it did not know what to do with it. Two ants were often seen tugging at the same piece for a long while; which was certainly a waste of time," etc., etc. It is the quality of *providence* in the ant, which is commended in Holy Scripture. The fact that, at least, some species of ants lay up a store for the winter, which Huber had denied, is now admitted beyond a doubt. I see in the ants, their restlessness, industry, their wealth of herds of aphides, slaves, soldiers, jealousies, battles, and the rest, a lively caricature of the vanities of human kind. An ant hillock, seems to me a very Vanity Fair in miniature!

b. Do birds sing *instinctively*?—It never occurred to me, for a moment, to doubt the fact, nor do I doubt it. But Mr Moggridge, in his interesting work on *Harvesting Ants* and *Trap-door Spiders*, has the following passage:—" Mr Wallace shews that there is some reason to doubt whether birds, which are so frequently said to build by instinct, would, under parallel circumstances, construct the nest proper to their kind; and he states that, birds brought up from the egg in cages do not do so, nor do they ever sing their parents' song without being taught." I suspect that Mr Wallace got his facts from a bird-fancier's shop, in which the instincts have not fair play. How can a canary build a proper nest in a wicker basket? His instinct would be only bothered by having half his work done to hand! Then, I believe, it is notorious that the chaffinch which builds in the suburbs of London does not make the exceedingly neat, pretty nest that we are familiar with, for the very good reason, that he cannot get the long, binding moss, which is found in rural districts. As to singing; in many a little town there is a thrush or skylark, not bought at a bird-fancier's, but reared from young by some boy—who would ever dream that the bird had to be *taught* to sing! It certainly is not the practice to teach them. As to those birds brought up in the fanciers' shops amongst a hundred others all singing, at once, different tunes, it is not wonderful they have to be taught to sing their native song. No instinct is indomitable, except those that support and procure life. Suppose a cock were hatched by steam, and kept aloof from other fowls—would he not crow? Absurd; I should as soon expect that he would grow no feathers.*

A happy new year to Proteus!   A.

* Since writing the above, an instance has come under my own notice which settles the question of the instinctive singing of birds to my complete satisfaction. Last summer, some friends in my neighbourhood took a young lark from the nest; and, since able to feed itself, it has been kept in a greenhouse, in the company of two canaries, two red, and one brown linnet, and, until recently, of a mocking-bird. It has now begun to sing, this spring, and, in spite of its noisy companions' different strains, it sings the song of its kind, though *it can hardly ever have heard a skylark sing.*—A.

LETTER XI.

AMADEUS TO PROTEUS.

Amadeus discourses on the Beautiful, and the insufficiency of Natural Selection to account for it. Its account is God.

MY DEAR PROTEUS,—I own that I find a difficulty in defining the beautiful to my satisfaction, though I know of several definitions. I must say as St Augustine says of time, "*Si non rogas intelligo.*" I will say, however, what the beautiful is not. And first it is not identical with the useful, or Darwin's theory would be equal to account for it. It is clear that an object may be very useful without being beautiful, or it may be beautiful without being useful. If the same object be at once both useful and beautiful, yet its beauty is not its utility; it is useful in one point of view, beautiful in another. The beautiful is not merely an agreeable association. The story of Beauty and the Beast does not require us to believe that the girl loved the monster for his brutal shape; though, by association, she regarded not his deformity, or indeed it became actually agreeable to her. I could almost say with Cousin, that beauty is unity in variety, did I not remember how, at Hennacomb, I could gaze for hours on the immeasurable reach of ocean, when its very monotony seemed to be a chief ingredient in its beauty.

Lastly, the beautiful is not that which is agreeable to the senses merely; for though the beautiful is always agreeable, yet the agreeable is not synonymous with the beautiful. Much more do I take exception to the beautiful being defined as, *what is agreeable to the senses*. This is what Proteus says (Letter v.), but I take it that he does not love to say it, and would be glad if I could make him unsay it. This is some of the philosophy of the Cavern of Despair. *La Théorie la plus grossière*, Cousin calls it; it is materialism pure and simple. Delicate meats and fragrant, sparkling wines create the sensation of the agreeable to the last extreme; but is this sensation identical with the sentiment of the beautiful? Is this the manner in which one is affected who contemplates a Madonna of Raphael, or the Apollo Belvidere, or a gorgeous sunset, or the "countless smile of ocean?"

I appeal from Proteus of the Cavern to Proteus the artist; is there no such thing as a *standard of the beautiful*? Is it absolute nonsense to speak of *an ideal*? But how should there be any standard, if the beautiful is that sensation by which each one is individually affected; or what has an ideal to do with sensation, further than that sensation is the *condition* of every mental experience? Musical notes are the condition of melody; but would it suffice to define a tune or melody as the combination of certain agreeable sounds? Such is the warbling of a bird, which however is not a tune or melody. There are persons who are music-deaf, and yet I suppose that they are affected by the same sensations, through musical sounds, by which we ourselves are affected; it is the *inward ear* which is deficient; it is denied them to appreciate certain relations of sound. And, I take it, there are men also who want, in great measure, the perceptions of certain relations in form and colour, in which the beautiful addresses itself to the mind through the sense of sight; or how shall I explain the grotesque taste of the savage, or the indifference of many persons to the charms of scenery?

What, in short, do I mean, when I say that a man has *bad taste;*—do I mean that his sensations are less keen than another's? I say that the man wants an intellectual gift; is either not endowed with it, or has not cultivated it. Proteus says, that men have learned to appreciate the beautiful in objects as they have learned to appreciate heat and cold; but I consider that this is just what marks the difference between sensation and the sentiment of the beautiful, that men do not *learn* to appreciate heat and cold; they are appreciated as soon as felt; whereas nothing is more capable of education than the eye and the ear for the perception of the beautiful in form or sound. Ruskin had to educate the people to appreciate Turner; and I should say that it would require an audience of musicians to appreciate Bach. I will undertake to prove the existence of God from the beautiful; but I cannot prove it to Proteus, if he abide by his definition.

If I were to say, that the beautiful consisted in certain harmonious relations, I should perhaps not go far astray, for order is earth's, as well as "heaven's first law;" but I might be perplexed if asked to state why certain relations were harmonious. Nor would the magnificent untuning of the elements in a storm at sea contradict this theory, for there is an order in that disorder; and, as in music, discords aptly disposed become concords. Without therefore defining in what the beautiful consists, I observe that there is one element in it, which I cannot think away without destroying the effect; and that is *law*. It may well be that, all which is according to law is not therefore beautiful; but, nevertheless, all that is beautiful must be according to law. Law, if not of the essence of the beautiful, must be an essential condition,—*sine quâ non*. I see law in nature's most random moods, in her greatest as in her minutest achievements. It is because law underlies the superficial irregularities of nature, that the artist can suggest a bush, or hedgerow, or a pool, or a pasture-field, by a few strokes of the pencil; while the untrained hand would, with many repeated efforts, produce an unmeaning confusion. In short, there is not, as Sir Thomas Browne observes, and never was, "Anything absolutely ugly, except chaos; in which every particle of matter is conceived as resting on its own centre, and out of relation with any other." As to your difficulty of realising chaos,—it would be very difficult for a man who had never been out of the tropics to realise ice, especially if he had never seen glass.

If then, it is law which has beautified the world, and law is the hand of God, it follows that nature is God's art; just in the same sense that music, or painting is man's art. But here Darwin's theory stands in my way, and I must dispose of it effectually, if I am to make good my argument.

As *advantage* is the chief feature in natural selection, I should expect, if Darwin's theory be of universal application, that the general aspect of nature would be similar to the aspect of a kitchen, or workshop. But it is not so. The rows of dish-covers, fire-irons, jacks, and candlesticks, in the one; and of planes, chisels, awls, hammers, and turnscrews, in the other, please me with their aptness and neatness; but the name of their quality is *fitness*, not beauty. Now in the general aspect of nature, it is, not fitness, but beauty which is the prevailing feature. And yet, there is fitness too, everywhere; but it is disguised, on the whole, with beautifulness. The beak of the puffin is a mere tool. Nature not being able, consistently with her plan, to make him a beauty, painted the beak and turned him out a droll. Yet, when I consider the matter more closely, I see that every bird's beak is as much a tool as the puffin's; but the beak of a merlin, or a parrot, or a kingfisher, suits so well with the general contour of the head and back, that one would think the divine Artist was guided solely by æsthetical considerations. And so it is with man's art; the buttress of a church is only a prop, but the architect makes me forget its vulgar use in its harmony with the other details of the structure. And everywhere, in the same manner, the useful is glorified by adornment; and then, there is to be considered that, in nature as in art, there are creations, like the flowers, which are simply beautiful for their own sake. Their only utility is their beauty: and you may well ask,—how is this? Why is the world so beautiful? The skeletal and muscular arrangements of man, which are the groundwork in the structure of the body, are merely calculated for usefulness; and, if man were accounted for solely on the principle of advantage, he might have wanted that exquisite beauty in himself, as well as that nice perception of it in others, without material detriment to his well-being. But here the theory of sexual selection stands in the way.

Although beauty be not absolutely necessary in the animal economy, yet, if it be only advantageous, natural selection would create it; and it is superfluous to recur, in this department, to the existence of God as the account of it. In accordance with this theory, "The peacock," Proteus observes, "owes to the brilliance of his plumage his very existence." Let this be so if it must; but mind, I will not believe it merely because Darwin's theory requires it. And, I must say, the facts adduced are not only impotent to bear the conclusion, but there is also very much to be said on the other side.

Darwin's theory requires, as to sexual selection, that brutes are to be accredited with a somewhat delicate appreciation of the beautiful in form, colour or sound. But, if what I have written here be true, the perception of the beautiful is an intellectual act! I know that, if I were to hold up the most lovely picture before a dog, he would be, intelligent as he is, utterly unmoved by it; and yet I am to think a tiger or leopard fastidious on the subject of stripes or speckles! I find it easier to realise chaos, than to realise that a wild beast is inspired with the sentiment of the beautiful! But as not fancy but argument must settle the matter, let us see how the case stands. Amongst the larger animals, the vigorous males would leave vigorous offspring; especially if to this vigour were added special weapons for combat in the males, which dispute with one another for the possession of the females. Here then one would expect that physical power would be the result; and that beauty would be nowhere. How then comes the lion with his kingly mane? How is it that the whole tribe of pards is gifted with such singular beauty? Amongst apes "the female is notoriously weaker," observes Mr Mivart, "and is armed with much less powerful canine tusks than the male;" and it is incredible that a female would often risk life, or limb, through her admiration of a trifling shade of colour, or a slightly greater, though irresistibly fascinating degree of wartiness." This writer considers that "Mr Darwin has utterly failed to show that sexual selection acts efficaciously in modifying species, *if indeed it acts at all.*" Then, there is the ugly fact of the exquisite colouring of certain shell-fish; where, fertilisation being effected by currents of water, selection by choice can have no place; and there is the case of the flowers, where it can equally have no place.

The account of the beauty of the plumage of birds, by sexual selection, seems more plausible, until one considers how exquisitely pretty are their eggs, studiously marbled, freckled, streaked, or spotted as they are. Surely there is a common origin for the beauty both of birds and eggs; which, in the latter case, can hardly be sexual selection, "The rock-thrush of Guiana, the bird of paradise, and some others, congregate," says Darwin, "and successive males display their gorgeous plumage and perform strange antics before the females, which standing by as spectators at last choose the most attractive partner." I have observed various antics and gambolings and flutterings of wing and tail, even amidst sparrows; but it never occurred to me that it was more than play. How is it then, that our dusky friend has not improved his plumage by it; while his cousin finch, the chaffinch, who, as I have observed, selects *by hard fighting*, is one of the gaudiest of his race? The gamecock, again, which for ages had his charms docked and trimmed for fighting, is a gaudy bird! But Mr Darwin's views on this head seem to have been met by a storm of remonstrance on the part of breeders and fanciers. Messrs Hewitt, Tegetmeier, and Brent, "well-known from their published works," "careful and experienced observers," " do not believe that the females prefer certain males on account of the beauty of their plumage." *

With regard to selection for song; I repeat what I have said,† that the song of birds, especially in its *fixedness* and *spontaneousness*, presents the character of an instinct. I find it difficult to believe that the birds have a greater nicety of ear and appreciation of their own song than have we who listen to them. I have heard them rivalling each other in their singing, in captivity; but only unbearable loudness and shrillness was the result. It certainly looks in favour of the theory that the best songsters are not conspicuous for their beauty; but then there is the gaudy goldfinch to be accounted for, on the other side; and how came that sweetly plaintive singer, the robin, with his red breast, or the mocking-bird with his jewelled eyes? I do not find anything in the animal world like what, with us, is the ear for music; though birds, and I

---

* Quoted from Mivart's "Genesis of Species."
† In my former letter.—A.

believe snakes, I know that lizards, are fond of musical sounds. Starlings, jays, and parrots can indeed be taught to whistle a tune; but it is a most mechanical affair. I am listening to one just now. He has, I observe, no conception of the melody as a whole; and he will whistle the phrase and antiphrase of the strain in a different key!

I think I have now finished with Darwin. If you think that I, who am no naturalist, have shown a certain want of modesty in differing from so weighty an authority, yet observe, that, as a rule, I have only seized on certain marked difficulties of the theory, which qualified writers have noticed, and on such as would occur to the most casual observer of patent facts; and lastly, I have had little confidence in him where he has least in himself. And if I have refused to believe that an abyss of wheels within wheels can be interpreted by a single formula, yet Darwin himself has yielded, on the question of its universality, and admitted, with that candour which is characteristic of him, that in his work on the Origin of Species, he *attributed too much to natural selection.*

And now, to return and to conclude with the theory of the beautiful with which I began: I am of the same persuasion with those writers who consider that ethical beauty is at the foundation of all beauty: I mean that colours, forms, or sounds, are not so much beautiful in themselves as rather the vehicles or channels by which certain spiritual attributes are suggested to our spirit. The figure of the lion is the embodiment of the ideas of gravity, power and majesty; the quality of a harebell is tender grace; the unbounded expanse of ocean mirrors the infinite.

In short, let a man attempt to describe any object whatever that is really beautiful, and his words will, on analysis, exhibit the most spiritual and transcendent ideas. The beautiful, considered from this point of view, is of infinite importance. I want to know what He is I am to win or lose for eternity? And I find that all the beauties of Nature are the expression of His attributes. Unity, variety, freedom, unchangeableness, grace, dignity, tenderness, symmetry, infinitude, peace, repose, power, order and other attributes, which are only contradictory because exhibited in broken lights in nature, but are one and harmonious in Him—what are all these but reflections of the Ancient Beauty, the Beautiful by which all things are beautiful?

Now I will define the word. The Beautiful is God; and what Newman says of music, in a passage well worth both quoting and meditating, I would apply, *mutatis mutandis*, to the beautiful in general. " Is it possible that that inexhaustible evolution and disposition of notes, so rich and yet so simple, so intricate yet so regulated, so various yet so majestic, *should be a mere sound* which is gone and perishes?' Can it be that those mysterious stirrings of the heart, and keen emotions and strange yearnings after we know not what, and awful impressions from we know not whence, should be wrought in us by what is unsubstantial, and comes and goes, and begins and ends with itself? It is not so; it cannot be. No; they have escaped from some higher sphere; they are the outpourings of eternal harmony in the medium of created sound; they are echoes from our Home; they are the voice of angels, or the Magnificat of saints, or the living laws of Divine Governance, or the *Divine*

Attributes; something are they besides themselves, which we cannot compass, which we cannot utter,— though mortal man, and he perhaps not otherwise distinguished above his fellows, has the gift of eliciting them."

Lastly, I have spoken of the *sentiment* of the beautiful: let us call it by its familär name, LOVE.— Your's affectionately, AMADEUS.

LETTER XII.

AMADEUS TO PROTEUS.

Evidences of the moral attributes of God. Why we should not look in the natural world for "mercy of a sentimental kind." The Future State. A boastful postscript.

MY DEAR PROTEUS.—I shall now take it for granted, I will suppose, at least for argument's sake, that there is a God who created and governs this visible order of things. The question next arises of the moral character (to use an inadequate expression) of such a Being. Now the moral character of God is shown in His government of the world. For as I set Revelation aside in the present argument, the only means we have of judging of His moral nature is by considering what is the system of His Government in the course of nature. For if there be a God, He is the Author of that system which we speak of as the course of nature. He appointed its rules, and presides over it, so that we are actually living under the government of God.

It has been said that "Nature *conceals* God and man reveals Him." Yet, I think, it is indisputable that, whatsoever account, or even if no account be given, of the existence and vast dominion of evil in the world, on the whole the general voice of nature proclaims a good, wise and beneficent Creator. For the general purpose of nature, in its plan and the laws of its development, looks towards and results in good; and this result is the more striking, to my mind, because it is evolved out of what appear to be evil and discordant elements. Thus, out of the seemingly random convulsions of natural forces comes the sidereal system—a world of order, light, and beauty out of chaos. The ruthless struggle for life amongst the brute creation results, and no doubt designedly,* in the perfection of species; as similarly out of the struggle of the various races of mankind emerges civilization; and, in manifold and divers other ways, good out of evil.† I think that this general tendency and progress of nature towards good is significant of its divine Author.

But, if from the mere outward creation and visible aspect of society, I turn to consider men themselves, as they are in their inward hearts, then indeed I find the most striking indication of those attributes of God, the evidence of which is in question between us. I find, with Butler in his Analogy, that, in this life, virtue is rewarded, distinctly *as* virtue, and vice punished *as* vice; not always indeed in the visible society of men, but what is immeasurably more important in the inward sanctions of conscience; and that while the criminal is made to " eat the fruit of

---

* A friend suggested to me that, "Since the struggle for life subserves an end, which need not follow (for mutual destruction might follow,) but does follow, viz., the perfection of species, is not this law a mark of design?"—A.

† "Not in each several portion of the work, but in the whole consists the admirable beauty of the Universe, in which even that which is called evil, being well-ordained and in fitting place disposed, doth more eminently commend the good." Aug. Enchiridion, chap. 10 et 11 *in prin. tom.* 3.—A.

his own way and be filled with his own devices," the just man is filled, as the very result of his goodness, with a peace and satisfaction of heart, which is one of the most pleasurable emotions of which our nature is capable. So that, if indeed there is a God, who is the Author of this moral scheme of things in which vice is ordained to be and to bring about its own punishment, He must Himself be moral, or righteous, whatever account be given of the existence of evil. His ordinances speak for themselves, commanding us to practise virtue and abstain from vice, as distinctly as if He shouted down His edicts from the skies.

It may be said, of course, that the materialistic theories of conscience and morality would annihilate the argument for a Moral Governor of the world, based on the sanctions of conscience and the moral quality of our deeds ; since, according to the latest fashion of ethical speculation, conscience is nothing but a subjective imitation of the action taken by society at large as to one course of conduct which it approves, as being eminently convenient, and an opposite course which it condemns and punishes, as eminently inconvenient to itself. But, why should I refute that which so ably refutes itself by explaining away, in its very statement, that which has to be accounted for ? By conscience nobody means a mental reproduction of the verdict of society ; and by morality nobody means that quality of our actions which society regards as practically convenient or inconvenient to itself. "I would not entertain a base design," one writes, "or an action that should call me villain, for the Indies ; and for this only do I love and honour my own soul, and have methinks two arms too few to embrace myself." * There speaks the conscience!

What has a sentiment of this kind to do with the convenience of society? Let us speak plainly; nothing is easier to explain on this materialistic theory, than conscience, or morality; *there is no such thing as one or the other.*

Unless, then, you wish me to consider this theory more attentively (for my own part I do not consider it worthy of such consideration) I simply set it aside as wrong in the very statement, and go on to conclude my argument thus :—

If, therefore, on the whole, the disposition and governance of the natural world points to a beneficent Author; if the facts of conscience plainly indicate that He is holy; if, as the rule, men find Him just and merciful in His providences towards themselves individually (though they may not see this in each particular instance) then, I say the existence of evil, whatever account be given of it, cannot gainsay the fact that God is good. Why Proteus himself, in the very act of questioning the justice and mercy of God, witnesses to the attributes which he questions. For, " He who planted the ear shall He not hear? And He who formed the eye doth He not consider?" And He who set in the heart of man justice and compassion, shall He not be just and compassionate? I can understand, then, how the fact of evil should have led men to say, that it was in the nature of things, and God Himself could not have prevented it; or that He was not absolute, but held divided empire with some malignant Spirit, who often thwarted Him,

* Sir Thomas Browne: RELIGIO MEDICI, prt. II., ch. 23.

and spoiled His plan; or that He permitted it, while hating it, for the sake of greater good ; but never that He Himself was not just and good.

And now, my dear Proteus, I address myself to your special difficulties and objections. You ask me "If I can furnish an instance in nature of mercy of a sentimental kind?" I do not know; but it seems to me that it is in God's dealings with the hearts and souls of men, and not in nature, that I should look for compassion of this sort. The world of nature is governed by laws, the violation of which, in the case of human beings, is accompanied by pain; and as the result follows mechanically and inexorably, mercy here is out of the question. Now, suppose the world governed, not by a system of laws, but by a system of interpositions, we can see that still greater evils would result, as Butler remarks. And I notice that such evils would be of a worse kind,—moral instead of physical. If, for instance, it seems dreadful that a man should suffer a life-long sickness in retribution for a criminal course of conduct, which he has long since repented of and amended, yet it would be far worse if men could always hope to be saved from the plain consequences of their evil deeds by some unforeseen interposition of sentimental mercy. In such a system, or rather absence of system, the very purpose of life as a state of discipline and probation would be frustrated.

For what is the purpose of life, since Proteus asks the question? What can be more plain from the consideration of the plan of nature, as governed by laws, the violation of which is followed by smart retribution in the shape of pain and anguish, than that life, as far as human beings are concerned, is a state of discipline and training towards perfection, especially as to those attributes of the nature of man in which he stands highest? What wiser or better institution of nature can we conceive, than that men living under a system of laws, should thereby be enabled to foresee the consequences of their actions as leading to happiness or misery; and that they should thus be taught, even by salutary violence, to act up to the light of reason, and attune their lives to the harmony of nature? Being opposed of its very nature to the will of man, what can strike so hard a blow at that irregular self-love, which is the root of moral evil, as pain? What more chastening to the spirit, when humbly and lovingly borne? And then, when we consider how closely allied in our present condition are pain and pleasure; that our sweetest joys are often born of tears; that we should hardly know what it is to be happy unless we had known what it was to suffer, I think we should hardly be surprised, if God, instead of abolishing evil, has taken it up into His scheme and ordained it to good.

Of course, the above remarks only, or chiefly, concern the case of those who suffer through their own fault. But to answer your objections as to the miseries of mankind at large, or the particular sufferings instanced by yourself, I should want to have the whole facts of the case. I must know the scheme as a whole, of which I only know a part. A child, on seeing the doctor bleed its father, might conclude the man to be a murderous villain; and I am just such a child in my ignorance of the Creator's purposes. But this I do see, that, supposing some distinct advantage is to be gained by the sufferings under consideration, (and such advantage is possible on the supposition of a future state for man and beast) the difficulty vanishes; for men make light enough of pain when some considerable though merely temporal advantage is to be gained by it. But what if such advantage be not temporal merely, but eternal? And such an hypothesis is not gratuitous, seeing that there is already positive evidence that God is good, and that His general plan in this life, as witnessed in His laws, is to effect the happiness of His creatures, and ordain evil unto good, notwithstanding the gloomy catalogue of accumulated miseries described in the bitter eloquence of Newman.

But the question as to the existence of a future state must be postponed for another letter. On the whole, I do not anticipate that, the existence of God and a future state once admitted, there will be further antagonism between us, as arising from the consideration of the evils of life. Proteus seems to say as much:—" It is easy to say that God is good; therefore there is no real injustice in the world ; and if He does not always hear our prayers, it is that we do not always know what is best for us. But, for this we must start with a belief in Him."—

Affectionately yours, AMADEUS.

P.S.—I am so slow by nature, and obliged to be still slower by circumstances, that I wonder you have patience with me. However the question of a future state will only occupy another letter. And then there is that grim creation of yours (well, not of yours, but of the materialists) to be dealt with,—I mean the Matter-God. Surely it was in bitter jest that you set him up! By God's help I will hew him hip-and-thigh; for I am sure you will be sadly disappointed if I don't. Then the controversy will be finished, I hope, so far as I at least am concerned. and so far as the matters embraced by our present programme extend. A.

LETTER XIII.

AMADEUS TO PROTEUS.

Metaphysical and moral proofs of Immortality. The existence of a Future State a sufficient answer to objections as to the miseries of the present life.

MY DEAR PROTEUS,—In order to approach my subject, I must go to the root of Immortality, which lies in the very nature of the soul itself. I shall therefore be obliged to be somewhat metaphysical; but I will endeavour to be as plain and brief as possible. What I have to say ought to have more weight, because it is not original, but merely the common-place wisdom of philosophy.

I find that I have a soul. I am so certain of this that to doubt it is not only absurd but impossible; for my soul is *myself*. I find, moreover, that my soul is not my body; for my body is *mine;* it is not *I*. I use the body, and the body is used by me. The eye cannot see, the ear cannot hear, of itself; but I use the eye or the ear, just as the eye itself uses a glass or the ear a deaf-trumpet, or the hand a staff. Hence I speak of the bodily faculties as organs, or instruments, with which I serve myself. Again, I know that my body is not myself, because it is constantly changing. Not an atom, even of my very bones, which is mine now, will be mine in twelve years time; but I—I remain. True I am changed, in one sense, at every moment; for I experience at every instant different feelings, desires, fancies, affections, and the rest; but it is the same *self* which experiences these changes, and connects them together. I am one, in the same, and identical in different times. I am not matter. For every particle of matter obeys the law of gravitation, which I resist at every moment, when I lift a hand or a foot, or turn my head. That which *resists* matter how can it *be* matter?* I am not matter, on this simple principle that one notion is not another notion, nor the same thing another thing. Matter is heavy, admits of shape, colour, size, of composition, dissolution; but I have thoughts, wishes, hopes, fears, regrets,—what has matter to do with such attributes as these? Or what have I in common with the qualities of matter? My body has them; and, for that very reason, it is mine indeed, but not I. To say that my soul is material then, is as contradictory as to say that matter is immaterial: it is unintelligible, or nonsense. †

Now, as I find myself to be a monad without parts, I cannot attribute to myself that dissolution which belongs to all things material and is called *death*. I am therefore naturally immortal. Death is simply the resolution of what is compounded into its constituent elements; and, as far as my body with its organs is concerned, it can have place, and must, as all experience shows, either by disorder, or the wear and

---

* Matter, in one respect, resists matter, but that is only *passively*, in what is called the *vis inertiæ*.—A.

† I have, throughout my letters, always used the term "unintelligible" in this sense, to designate, not what is merely *incomprehensible*, but what is absolutely *unthinkable*.—A.

tear of daily use; but, as I am conscious that my bodily organs are not I who use them, how can their decay eclipse *me*? The destruction of the *self*, or person, is not implied in the notion of death; but only the destruction of that mechanism, and those organs which unite me to, and render it possible for me to communicate with, the world around me. How I shall fare when these instruments, muscles, brain, nerve-centres, refuse to obey the will, and are unfit for vital functions, I know not; but of one thing I must be sure, that, however their loss may affect me, it cannot make me cease, any more than the musician ceases to be one, because he has lost his instrument. If I am *partless*, to say that I can die is contradictory or unintelligible; and what perishes is only a machine; for the body, however exquisitely contrived, is nothing more.

How I came into existence, unless God created me, I know not; nor how I should cease to exist, unless He blot me out with the finger of His *Fiat*, I know not; but such a blotting out would not be what we call death, but annihilation. Such annihilation is doubtless as possible with God as creation; but I doubt whether it ever occurred to any one seriously to apprehend destruction in this manner. As there is no instance given in experience of such annihilation, it is hard even to realise it; and men are not affected by what they cannot realise. No man, on lying down to rest, doubts but that, when he wakes in the morning (if he wake at all), the sun and earth, and the other orbs will be in their proper places: it is but the ordinary course of nature. If any one were to tell him that he could not logically prove that this would be so, he would only smile; because he would know that a practical certainty was as good as logic for the uses of life; and he would be right. Besides the notion of annihilation being unpractical, it would, I think, argue God of some deficiency of resources, that he should create, only to blot out again, so many millions of gifted creatures! I am not surprised, therefore, if the heathen philosopher should have regarded Immortality as a certainty; and that one chapter of the *De Senectute* of Cicero[*] should read like Thomas à Kempis; for, putting aside the metaphysical proof, there is a voice within the secret chamber of the heart which cries aloud, *Non omnis moriar*, more eloquently than rhetoric itself; the very apprehension of Immortality is an argument for it. And then there are those other moral arguments, such as the unequal distribution of the goods and prizes of life, the wrongs which require redress, and the ills which demand compensation. This sort of argument is better, perhaps, than metaphysical proof, in which I might suspect some secret flaw; but the voice of nature is the voice of God. Putting all these considerations together, I regard Immortality (setting revelation aside) not so much as a matter of speculation as a matter of fact.

[*] "O præclarum diem, quum ad illum divinum animorum concilium cœtumque proficiscar, quumque ex hac turbâ et colluvione discedam! Proficiscar enim non ad eos solùm viros, de quibus antè dixi; sed etiam ad Catonem meum, quo nemo vir melior natus est, nemo pietate præstantior: cujus a me corpus crematum est, quod contra decuit ab illo meum. Animus verò non me deserens, sed respectans, in ea profectò loca discessit, quò mihi ipse cernebat esse veniendum: quem ego meum casum fortitèr ferre visus sum: non quòd æquo animo ferrem; sed me ipse consolabar, existimans non longinquum inter nos digressum et discessum fore." *De Senectute*, chap. xxiii. Confer *Imitation*, Bk. iii., chap. 48.

I find, moreover, that there are several sorts of souls. That the brutes have souls is as certain to my mind as that I have a soul myself. A man must be very dull, not to see that the same arguments which prove an immaterial, immortal principle in ourselves prove the same for the brutes. Cardinal De Cusa, Cudworth, Butler, Balmes,* and I dare say others, have noticed this: it is indisputable. A brute, though it is not a person, possesses those attributes of unity, individuality, and identity which are at the base of personality. It is not by a mere figure of speech, that I speak of a dog or cat, as *he* or *she*, that I give them a name, and say that they think and feel, and love those who are kind to them. Their minds are certainly different from our own, not only in degree, but in kind. I suppose Aristotle is right

* De Cusa assigns an hereafter to the souls of brutes in the Anima Mundi. *De Ludo Globi*, Lib. 1.

Cudworth considers that if, after death, such souls transmigrate into other bodies, this is only what one witnesses daily, in the actual course of nature, in the case of the silk-worm and other such grubs. *Intellectual System*, Part 1., Bk. 1., ch. 5.

Bishop Butler argues that, if the immortality of brutes implied "that they must arrive at great attainments, and become moral agents, even this would be no difficulty, since we know not what latent powers and capacities they may be endued with;" but he adds that "the natural immortality of brutes does not in the least imply that they are endued with any latent capacities of a rational, or moral nature; and the economy of the universe might require that there should be living creatures without any capacities of this kind." *Analogy*, Part 1., ch. 1.

Balmes speaks to much the same purpose: "We know not of what use they would be; but we may conjecture that, absorbed again in the bosom of Nature, they would not be useless . . . . Who says that the vital principle residing in brutes can have no object, if the organisation which it animates be destroyed?" *Fundamental Philosophy*, Bk. ii., ch. 2. It is only fair to add, however, that this writer does not coincide with my condemnation of the supposition of annihilation.—A.

in saying that the difference consists in this, that the brutes only know particulars; however I observe that my parrot uses a concrete word so as to give it a generic force, in the same way that infants do.* For the rest, the mind of a brute is like our own. As they have no general notions, they should be unable to reflect or make a proposition; but they have feelings, associations, and affections. They are capable of improvement within their own sphere to an indefinite extent. And if any one shall say that such qualities and endowments are accountable for without the supposition of a soul, then have I none myself. That scriptural phrase "the beasts that perish" must be so explained as not to contradict the speculation of the Wise Man, as to the upward or downward destination of the life of the beast, when he dies;† nor that affirmation of St Paul that, not only "ourselves," "who have the first fruits of the spirit," but "every creature ‡ groaneth and is in labour ... waiting for the adoption of the sons of God." To say that a brute has a soul, and to say that he is immortal, is to say the same thing.

I spoke with one the other day who was averse to this notion of immortality on the part of the brutes, as being an odd conceit. His own was, that God had

* *Anything eatable* he calls *cheese*.—A.

† "Who knoweth if the spirit of the children of Adam ascend upward, and if the spirit of the beasts descend downwards?"—according to the Vulgate. Eccles. iii. 21. The Hebrew has, "who knoweth the spirit of the sons of Adam that goeth upward, and the spirit of the beast that goeth downward to the earth?" The difference, which is a matter of vowel pointing in the Hebrew, does not affect my argument. The word spirit (which is רוּחַ here, not נֶפֶשׁ) is the same for the soul both of man and beast.—A.

‡ Πᾶσα ἡ κτίσις; *the whole creation*.—A.

so contrived the union of soul and body in the brute, that on the death of the latter, the former naturally perished ; but, on my reminding him that God Himself could not do that which was unintelligible or contradictory, he then had recourse to the conceit of annihilation ;—so often as a man crushes a beetle or a gnat, or slaughters a sheep, God takes occasion to blot out the immortal life by an act of omnipotence. Thus, did he think God was employed in perpetually undoing His own work, by a series of miraculous interpositions. And yet, it were a less evil that the whole material universe should be destroyed throughout the immeasurable expanse of space, than that a single living, thinking, loving creature should perish.*

I say that it is this conceit of annihilation which is the odd conceit. There is no warrant for it in nature, reason, or in Scripture; it is purely gratuitous, and equally unworthy of the Almighty and of commonsense.† Moreover, it must be a dreadful doctrine to hold, for one who has a feeling heart, considering how many deaths men are thus answerable for, through wanton sport, or anger, or heartlessness and indifference. I assure you, that this view of the case saddened my sport, when I was a child : for though

* St Augustine admires the soul of a fly, which, he says, far transcends light, or any, the most exquisite materia. *Op. Edit. Ben.*, Vol. viii. p. 78.—A.

† Had the rule of our controversy admitted of re-casting this letter for publication, I should certainly have somewhat subdued the *violence of expression*, as to my deeply rooted conviction of the immortality of brutes; but this, observe, merely as a matter of taste. For if the reader consider what is here said on that subject, apart from the manner of saying it, I have hardly gone beyond the grave and cautious Bishop Butler.—A.

I felt as if it were a wicked thing to do, I could not refrain from the slaughter of small perch. "Why should you take away that life which you cannot give?" was a saying of my betters; and I was simple enough to believe them, that God had put this awful power in my hands, of dealing around me that annihilation, which, in the judgment (I believe) of St Thomas Aquinas, is worse than damnation. One sentence of Butler rid me, long ago, of this silly superstition. And I thank God, I now know, to my great comfort, that I cannot *really kill* even a gnat: I can only destroy that material organism through which the life manifests itself; the life itself I cannot touch. What happens to that life, when, through act of mine, it has been freed from its little prison-house? Shall it germinate again—run through a thousand cycles by turns "as beast or bird or fish or opulent flower?" Who knows what it is, what its hidden worth may be, what latent capacities it may be endowed with? Is the law of development confined to "this little green planet?" "These things were all made for man's use and benefit," it will be said. Good; but God may have a hundred ends in view, as well as one, in their creation; and they may still benefit other men, or other beings, through all ages, for aught we can say to the contrary. I firmly believe that there is no waste in nature; that not the least drop of life will be spilt. The dust returns unto its dust, and the spirit to God who gave it. He will see that it suffer no injury from my wantonness—no, nor real disadvantage of any kind.

From this high vantage ground of Immortality, I make light of even so considerable a matter as physical pain. It never occurred to me, as a child, to pity *Indur*,[*] in Mrs Barbauld's beautiful story, who, in the course of his transmigrations, must so often fall into the bitterness of the agonies of death. Such a trifle is not worth the reckoning, in comparison of so brilliant a career as the fairy Perezinda had ordered for him. Our larger sympathy, no doubt, vastly exaggerates the sufferings of the brute beasts; and, even in human suffering, when at its extreme degree, it is not "corporal sufferance," but "apprehension" that unmans us; as Shakespeare remarks, in that celebrated passage which everybody quotes and almost everybody misunderstands.[†] But, waiving all such considerations, and allowing even that the sufferings of man or beast are really great, in themselves, as they seem in apprehension, yet what does it all amount to when viewed in the light of eternity? One who has an everlasting career in prospect may well put up with an occasional "bad quarter of an hour"—for such, or less, will the longest period appear to immortal eyes. It may well be that the pains and heartaches and misfortunes, the scorns, contumelies, and fardels of life, are, in the eternal scheme, blessings and advantages of the same nature as are

[*] The *Transmigrations of Indur*: Evenings at Home.

[†] Who would think, from the manner in which the passage about the *beetle* and the *giant* is usually quoted, that Isabella, urging Claudio to die, *makes equally light of the corporeal agony both of man and insect?*

"—— Darest thou die?—
The sense of death is most *in apprehension;*
And the poor beetle that we tread upon,
In *corporal sufferance* feels a pang as great
As when a giant dies."
—*Measure for Measure.*—A.

rank, health and fortune in the estimation of men;*
so that the young lady, with her sad, chronic earache,
is more to be envied than Proteus who pities her?
but supposing they are not so, does it matter, if
"all the sufferings and afflictions of this life are not
worthy to be compared with the glory that shall be
revealed in us?"

What I say of individual sufferings, I say also of
the disorders of society at large; though the world
be ever so full, like the prophet's scroll, of lamentation and mourning and woes. If this world be a
scheme complete in itself, the objections of Proteus
are unanswerable; but if the career of man be only
the fragment of an eternal scheme, we must know
the scheme as a whole, to be able to judge of it. If
the ways of God are ever fully to be vindicated to man,
there must be a *General Judgment*. Affectionately
yours, AMADEUS.

* This answer to the difficulty of physical evil occurs in "Morbegno," a poem in the January number (I think) 1876 of *Macmillan's Magazine*; but, after all, the writer only reasserts, in poetic phrase, the doctrine of the Beatitudes.—A.

LETTER XIV.

AMADEUS TO PROTEUS.

Amadeus a bad controversialist. He becomes the disciple of Proteus! Strange fecundity of Space, and a world self-created out of Nothing! The Matter-God in jeopardy. "How shall we shape our lives?"—Catastrophe!

MY DEAR PROTEUS,—Your last letter to me concludes with a quotation of certain words of mine, which I now wish to retract. "But enough of this" (you had been laying the ground plan of a system of materialism)—" enough of this," you write, "which I am afraid is *just the talk with which you find it difficult to keep patience*—you must, however, try to do so." I will. Why, I have broken the very pledge I made at the start of the controversy—that I would endeavour, not to refute, but convince you! And, in my last letter but one, speaking of the Matter-God, I so far forgot my modesty, as to swear that *I would hew him hip-and-thigh!* I am afraid that I am proving, in the worst sense of the word, *a bad controversialist.*

Besides, what had you said to shock me?—" I shall be doing no more than is called for of me, if I state, in terms, the alternative to which the rejection of God, the Creator, reduces me."—Exactly; and would not such rejection reduce *me* to the same alternative? Why, then, should I rend my garments? Have with you, my Proteus! Where you go I will go. I said that I would explore with you this gloomy cavern, and I am going to be as good as my word. You have constructed the skeleton of the Matter-God; and, I begin to see, with a wise purpose. I am going, with the same purpose, to clothe him with flesh, and set his god-ship on his legs. I don't think that this is a sort of spectacle such as that Gorgon, which confronted Dante and his ghostly guide amongst the Shades, and from which they had to hide their eyes, lest the sight should turn them to stone.* I shall, instead, bid you look this thing straight in the face.

One word more by way of preface. You may be at first tempted to think that, in the work which I have cut out for myself, I am only playing with the subject, and trifling with yourself. But by such a suspicion you would wrong me. I wish, like you, *merely to contemplate the alternative to which I should be driven by the rejection of theism.* Now then, I sit at your feet.

Matter then is the self-existent being; therefore matter must be infinite. The inference is just. For what is there to limit it? We cannot say that as it necessarily exists so it is necessarily limited; for that same divine necessity which determines it to be cannot at the same time fetter or hinder its being;

---

* See "INFERNO," Canto ix. 52, where the poet intimates that, under the symbol of Hell, he is describing the horrors of such a cavern as Proteus and I are groping in :—

" O voi, ch'avete gl'intelletti sani,
Mirate la dottrina che s'asconde
Sotto 'l velame degli' versi strani."

One meets only too many people who have seen the Gorgon.—A.

this would be contradictory, unintelligible. "Twy-nature is no nature," quoth the poet, and *à-fortiori*, twy-essence is no essence; equally impossible and unthinkable. Matter then is everywhere, for the same reason that it is anywhere; or rather, all place is in it. It is in all time for the same reason that it is in any time; or rather, all the successive points of time are in it, and itself is eternal.

But here a difficulty occurs which has not escaped the careful eye of Proteus. To say that matter is everywhere, is not true, surely, if by matter we understand that which exists after the mode of extended, divisible particles; for where is matter in an exhausted receiver? Besides, it is clear that concrete matter can be neither self-existent nor infinite, from the very reason of the thing,—else why should not this pebble choke up the universe? since, according to the foregoing reasoning, as 'self-existent it should be everywhere, for the same reason that it is anywhere. Nay, were concrete matter infinite it would annihilate space itself; since there cannot be two infinities, and space is certainly infinite—if, that is to say, it is really anything.

But matter has at least one attribute of infinitude; it is infinitely divisible, says Proteus. I once thought so myself, until I reflected on the manifold, palpable contradictions which such a statement involves. Matter, to be infinitely divisible, must consist of an infinite number of extended parts, as the very capability of such a division. According to this view, a single pebble would choke up the universe; since it is infinitely divisible, and therefore consists of an infinite number of extended particles, which would make it to be of infinite bulk, however small such particles might be, since there must be an infinite number of them, as the capability of an infinite division.*

"But," you might say, "it can be mathematically demonstrated that matter is infinitely divisible." I was once dumbfounded by this objection; but I know now the trick that was played upon me; and that what the mathematician pretended to divide, with the notional sword of a breadthless line, was not concrete matter, but pure space! Again there is surely the same kind of fallacy in asserting that matter is compounded of the compounded *ad infinitum*—as in asserting that there are causes *ad infinitum* to the denial of a First Cause. The only account of the compound is the simple; just as the only account of the plural is the singulars which go to make it up. But the statement which assigns infinite divisibility to matter bristles with contradictions in its every aspect. It would make the part equal to the whole; since each part is infinitely divisible into further parts, and the whole itself cannot be more than infinitely divisible. Instead of one, we should thus name a myriad of infinites; besides that, an infinite number is itself unintelligible. The true notion of the infinite transcends number; just as it also transcends place.

Perhaps you will be surprised that I deal so minutely with a statement in itself of so little importance. Nor indeed should I care to, had I not a set purpose

---

* Proteus might retort that, if a pebble ought to fill the Universe, so an inch ought to be as long as a mile, since it includes an infinite series of spacial intervals.—Ed.

in so doing. I wish to show that it is, not concrete matter, but SPACE which is the *Primum Philosophicum* of Proteus. And I think Proteus himself sees that it is so. "All the researches of astronomy," he writes, "fail *to discover a limit to space*, or of the luminous bodies which compose the heavens." The arguments for the infinitude of matter would be weak without space. For it does not follow that because man has failed to number the stars that they are therefore innumerable, or that, because the eye and the microscope present matter as divisible, that it is therefore infinitely divisible. But space is the real self-existent, infinite, unchangeable of Proteus. We cannot annihilate space even in thought; though we can easily suppress the existence of objects in space—even our own existence; and this incapacity of annihilation is the very characteristic note of a necessary notion.

Again, if we say that matter is infinite, the infinitude is not attributable to the same thing, but to an aggregate which is composed of different things; so that there is a fallacy in the very assertion; but space is no aggregate. Hence, too, it is only by a figure of speech that one calls it infinitely divisible; for it is more invulnerable than the air. Space then is infinitely extended, and, if it be correct to say that it can be divided, it is infinitely divisible; it is eternal, unchangeable, without beginning or end—if only it be real. I start from space, then, and out of space I propose by evolution, to construct the universe!

I own it appals me to think of the frightful abyss of nothingness from which I have to start in my philosophy. The very contemplation of this awful void scares and makes me dizzy. And then, for I was ever addicted to extremes, an opposite feeling comes into play, and I am inclined to laugh at my scheme as utterly absurd and ridiculous, a mere whimsey, most like the dream of a lunatic, to make a world out of nothing! But what other alternative is left me, if I deny the existence of a supra-mundane God? Space—why it seems, as I just now said, identical with nothing. It is a mere void, the absolute negation and contradictory opposite of existence. Its very necessity seems only of a merely negative character. It is of necessity *nothing*: it is infinitely opposed to that which is. It seems only indirectly thinkable, as the negation of that which is extended. It is the absence of light, life, form, and substance, and all that is congenial to thought as realities kindred to itself. It is a mere relation, an *ens rationis* ——.

But I must not say this; for, unless I allow a reality to space, how can I account for anything? An account of the universe there must be; and in default of God, space is the account. But because it baffles my understanding, I will call in imagination to my assistance. The uncultivated savage might view the vault of heaven as just such a vacuum as space; but to the eye of science it is filled with that subtle fluid, the air, which is the nourishment of life. Again —a still better illustration—the soul, itself invisible and intangible, is more real, if possible, than the body; for it causes the body to be what it is, a *living* body. Space then may be real, in spite of its being impalpable, invisible, and, in itself, unthinkable.

Space is real then, and all reality has to be evolved out of it. But before I proceed to the first phase of this necessary evolution, I must know precisely what evolution is.

Evolution, I conceive, is an *unfolding* of one phase into another phase of existence, whether of similar or dissimilar aspect. And it is a primary canon of such evolution (for it is a law of thought, *ex nihilo nihil fit*) that what is evolved must be virtually contained in that from which it is evolved. I think, though this be self-evident, it is worth the stating, for some persons do not realise it: they speak as if anything could be evolved out of anything, which is absurd.* Now for an illustration of the matter.

There used to be a fellow (perhaps there is now somewhere or other) who would make the people gape at a country fair by cramming his mouth with a heap of tow or paper shavings, and then pulling out therefrom the particoloured semblance of a barber's pole. This would seem a kind of miracle, did not one reflect that the barber's pole must have existed already in another form, furled up in the tow or shavings. That is a real evolution; and all evolution must be like it, if we would talk sense. And Nature's evolution is like it. For how can a live chicken come out of an egg? Why, because the chicken is already virtually there.

* I find I am anticipated, in this very obvious remark, by a passage in that clever satire, "The New Republic";—

"'When we realize,' says Mr Stockton, 'when we truly make our own this stupendous truth' [that, all that is has evolved itself from a brainless, senseless, lifeless gas, and that it may one day return to it] 'must not our feelings at such moments be religious? Are they not *Religion ?*'

"'But,' said Miss Merton, 'there is nothing religious *in* a gas. I don't see how anything religious can come out of it.'

"'Perfectly right!' chuckled Mr Saunders, faintly clapping his hands. '*Nothing can come out of the sack but what's in it.*'"—A.

For see, the egg is alive, if it be a fresh egg; and the proof of this is, that it takes just double the time to freeze a fresh that it takes to freeze a stale egg. The life has to be killed in the former before the freezing can commence; but the latter is dead already, and so freezes at once. In like manner, had I microscopic eyes, I doubt not but I should see the young tadpole in the fertilized spawn of the frog, and the oak-tree lying furled up in the acorn. Nor do I marvel, this being so, that a single grain should become a wheat-field. I am not staggered at the *Acarus Crossii* of the *Vestiges*, nor do I smile incredulous if science tells me that man himself can produce vitality by a certain adjustment of chemical agents and affinities—he produces it, I say, in this sense, that he merely disengages the life which slumbers in the chemical ingredients.

With this proviso, I pass on to the first phase of evolution. Matter, life, plant, fish, bird, mammal, man—God himself can be evolved out of pure space, on one condition, *that they be therein contained*. It is a startling assertion, but I leave wonder to children. *Nil admirari* must ever be your motto in philosophy: what more mysterious than the very fact of existence! But, while I part with wonder, I cannot part with common sense. Unless the universe be virtually contained in space evolution is unintelligible.*

---

* If any one should suspect that this argument of Amadeus, against the self-evolution of the *universe*, might be turned against the Christian doctrine of Creation out of nothing, yet I think we have in the comparison of the two statements a very good instance of the difference between an absurdity and a mystery. That the void of nothingness should *evolve itself* into existence is a sheer contradiction; but that a living, infinite Power should create a world out of nothing is indeed

Space evolves itself into an immense ocean of molecules, thicker than the motes in the sunbeams, the mere fluff or sundust of which our planet, and by analogy the whole sidereal system, is composed. This is the first concrete matter, which, submitted to analysis, results in *carbon, oxygen, hydrogen,* and *nitrogen.* I say, space thus evolves itself by the same inherent law of its nature by which it exists at all. The infinite manifests itself, not as another infinite, which would be unintelligible, but as somewhat, in its vast immensity, emulous of infinitude ; for who shall count the stars or the sands of the sea ?

" Give me matter and motion," Descartes is reported to have said, "and I will create the universe." To attribute movement to pure space would seem unintelligible. But we have done with speculation for the present. That movement belongs to concrete matter is a fact.

This whole sidereal system starts from a vast vortex of sun-dust, the fruitful sperm of things, which coagulating in the centre, and molten by the friction of motion at a white heat, first flattens at the poles, then bursts, or sloughs, and sheds suns, planets, moons, or rings through the infinite reaches of space. Science gives our planet first to view as an ocean of molten granite, detached from its sun, and revolving on its own axis. The gross steam which arises from its surface condenses as it comes into contact with the

incomprehensible as to the *modus operandi,* but involves no contradiction, and therefore no impossibility. Those who fancy that it does must suppose "nothingness" to be a *quasi*-material out of which God created the Universe. The expression simply means that the Creation was a *creation,* and not merely an organisation out of existing matter.—ED.

cold, whence it descends again in everlasting rains, which, brought again into contact with the heated surface, hiss forth in fresh streams which ever darken the sun.

But in this impenetrable horror of gloom, heat and vapour the foundations of the earth are laid. For vast hot rivers are melting the granite, as it crusts, and pouring it into the lowest levels (which are fast becoming seas) to make the first stratified rocks. Gradually, but through what vast æons of time who shall tell? the land rises up, the ocean lashes the strand, whereon as yet is no breath of light (the heat forbids), nor plant, nor animal. And gradually again, but still, through lapse of ages, the surface cools of sea and land; a wan light pierces the clouds, and, by what happy, fortuitous concurrence of ingredients I know not, the chemic travail has begun, and the first spores are quickened in the womb of nature into anelid or fucoid,—lowest forms, sponge, sea-fungus, coral, and the fish that has the skeleton outside. But ever and anon, the untamed central fires rend the crusted surface, invade the land or sea with ocean streams of boiling lava; and huge land-slips and fierce volcanoes threaten the return of ancient chaos. Then these subside once more, and the air unloaded of its moisture by huge growths of gigantic ferns, the result of universal tropic heat, the glorious sun bursts forth, and shines on a creation strange and monstrous to our experience, now sealed in the rocks. Strange wombats, huge hog-like labyrinthodons, pterodactyl, ichthyosaurus, plesiosaurus, monster fowls and elephantine beasts.

In vain; creation, after creation, is swept away

by vast and universal cataclysms. The earth contracts (at first huger than itself with its own heat) and contracting rends its hide; whence land and sea often change places; and last, a universal winter whitens the world for ages.

This, its cause unknown, at last upbreaks, and vast rivers prepare the soil for that noblest of *Simiæ*, whose hand and brain, of nature's subtle and most curious workmanship, and upright gait have made him lord of all. First a brute, no better than his kind, "butting his brother brute for lust or provender;" but last, improved by breed and circumstance, or use, or the struggle of life, or the mere caprice of evolution in the vital force, or all combined, he begins to hurl a stone, to fashion a rude weapon.—From that day he is lord of all. Weaker in brute violence than his enemies, he herds for safety with his kind. Intercourse sharpens his already superior sagacity. His jabberings are becoming articulate sounds and signs, which necessity perfects into the rudiments of a language. He learns to cook his food, to clothe his naked body with furs and hides, and other simple arts of savage life.

Law soon becomes a necessity of his social life: to this his own selfishness prompts him with precocious sagacity; for individual unrestraint turns at last to the ruin of the individual himself. Hence all conspire against the unruly offender. Law manifests itself in the institution of tribes, nationalities and commonwealths, and at last engenders the ideas of vice and virtue. The first virtues, as we learn from early records, being reverence for the elders, or *piety*, manhood, and hardihood (*virtus*), patriotism, honesty and truthfulness, and self-restraint; and the opposites of these are the chief vices. Thus conscience is created, which, first the mere apprehension of the vengeance of society, through habit is fixed in the mind, independent of the motive which created it. Meantime the imagination has kept pace with the progress of the reason, or rather outstripped it. The movements of nature suggest an unseen worker (for the idea that matter itself is alive, with the life of evolution, is a nafter-thought of science). Hence, the heavenly bodies, the land, sea, mountain, and stream are peopled with genii, naiad and oread, gods and goddesses innumerable. These, at length, are either superseded by, or rendered subordinate to one Sovereign Being of rare and transcendent attributes—the noblest creation of the imagination of man; until, after the lapse of ages, reason annuls the creations of imagination by exposing the true history of their origin. Man himself is God, and Public Opinion the mouthpiece by which He speaks, the great and common educator, the umpire of vice and virtue, the suppressor of creeds and superstitions, the terror of evil-doers, the fosterer of peace, concord, progress, and humanity.

Here, my Proteus, is our God! Regard him well. His head is of fine gold, his breast and arms are silver, his belly and thighs of brass, his legs of iron, his feet of dirt—or nothingness. But, indeed, though a flimsy glory circle round his brow, if you but touch him, he will crumble into dust. Head, bust, belly, legs and feet, he is wholly dirt. Why demolish that which must soon perish of its own inherent rottenness? Nor can I say, nor does it much matter, whether his natural decay will first set in at head or foot;—or is this latest fashion of civilization to be immortal, rather than that of Greece or Rome? But grant it so: what is civilization but an abstraction? The individual shall soon return into his component gases, whether society progress or retrograde; and society is only composed of individuals. Neither Dives in fine linen, nor Lazarus in rags and ulcers, can escape the common doom. But, if he perish not at head, this Matter-God, I momently tremble for his safety at foot. I mean that the very existence of this material globe is every day in jeopardy. A fault in the earth's crust might yawn and engulf the sea, and burst up our planet like a bombshell.

Judge now if this be a mad fancy of mine. The history of our globe, if there be truth in the sermons of the stones, is replete with such catastrophes. The tops of the highest mountains have been under water, not once, but many times: sea and land have often changed places.

Twenty-nine creations, it is asserted, have already perished, and I daresay this figure is under the mark. The great fauna of the Glacial Period must have perished instantly, for their flesh was found uncorrupted in the ice-blocks, and was eaten by dogs of our period! The centre of the earth glows with more than furnace heat. At a depth of two miles water, at a depth of thirty iron itself, would be at boiling heat. The earth will still split and crack and crumple in the cooling process, as it has split and cracked and crumpled heretofore. Are not Etna, Vesuvius, and the Geysers solemn facts? Why should this creation alone be spared? Is man not mere dirt like the mastodon?

Does it not concern Proteus that the sun itself is cooling? for those telescopic spots are surely vast tracks of land-crust, could we neighbour them to see. Do you see how that star in Charles's Wain has begun to dim and sicken even in our day? That little group of planets in our system, are they not fragments of a huger ruptured globe? But indeed we need not pass, for examples, beyond the dead worlds entombed beneath our feet. The earth is doomed; and man himself, society and individual, emptied of his glory, shall pass into the draff of sun-dust—in that very nothingness of empty space from whence he sprung.

These things being so, how are we affected by them? What shall be our religion? How shall we shape our lives? Shall we grovel and eat dirt? Never—God or no God, depend upon it, vice is a mistake. Virtue is the spring of reverence, without which some nobler spirits would hardly live, or live a blighted life; but others prefer pleasure, even at the sacrifice of virtue. For me, I think I should choose me out some worthier being of our kind, and reverence myself that he might reverence me, and keep myself clean in thought and act for his sake, so far as frailty would allow. For as to this civilization, it seems to me but a sorry mockery of those perfections which our simple forefathers assigned to God.—What think you of love and friendship, and the social board, and the flash of wit, and music, and merriment? But all in due bounds; for there are those who have squandered, like the prodigal, their very capital of pleasures, in riotous living, and have lost the very capacity of enjoyment. Besides, pleasure is only thoroughly enjoyed by him who has deserved it by honest hard work. But what is to become of the *wretch* who can neither work nor enjoy? I own that, when my brain is overwrought, nay, if but my head ache, or a nerve thrill with anguish, I shun my fellows, lest my griefs should jar with their healthy humours; and were such grief lasting none would love me, and I should loathe myself and my life. What then but "a stout heart, a ladder, and a rope!"

This certain cure society forbids—by what right, if there be no God?

That old French general who, when his banker failed and ruined him, straightway blew out his brains, did surely a sensible thing: how should he change his habits at his time of life? I say, if society dislike suicide, let it shut our mouths, and keep it ever a dead secret that *there is no God*. Let it not be whispered in the dark! There are so many wretches —why I myself, in certain sad moments, have prayed the good God, for sweet mercy sake, to make an end.—And then *it is so easy to do it*, it seems nothing should baulk a man who is that way given.

There is another thought which must make way in the Godless era we are inaugurating, though it will be violently opposed at first. Why cherish we our sickly children—the epileptic, the idiot, the consumptive, the halt and hump-backed? Why tolerate the unseemly childishness of age? And wherefore the ghastly horrors of the work-house, the hospital and the lunatic asylum? Perish the sickly sentiment of relatives who would keep these living corpses above ground because, forsooth, *they love them!* Back with them into their sun-dust out of which they have made so sinister an evolution, and let quick-lime hasten the process! What! this world is for youth! Shall our cups and songs be tainted with memories of the charnel-house!

* * * * * *

But after penning these ungentle sentiments, I fall into a lethargy. Methinks that time is the merest illusion—an order of succession not of duration. The end is at hand.—Then an explosion, the noise of which itself would have killed me, could I die, wrenches me from the body, and shoots me into the void,* but a Voice awful and calm says: "ARISE YE DEAD AND COME TO JUDGMENT."—Affectionately yours, AMADEUS.

(*To be continued.*)

* The earth *bursts*. A fault in the thin crust (only thirty miles!!) lets the sea through amongst the central furnaces: the steam thus created rends the earth. This is a mode of the final catastrophe very familiar to my fancy.—A.

LETTER XIV. *(continued.)*

AMADEUS TO PROTEUS.

Amadeus reviews his argument, and concludes.

THE object of my last unfinished letter, was to see if our theory of the deification of matter would bear a thorough statement. With this purpose in view, I supposed it a true theory and strove conscientiously to render it as intelligible as possible; but I think with indifferent success. I could not, in fact, conceal from myself the enormous difficulties under which I was labouring; and these increase as I look back to consider calmly what I have written. Space being the true infinite in our theory, I ask, What is space? If a non-entical void, shall I, like Hegel, identify absolute Being with nothing? This is the sheerest contradiction. If however, I suppose, that there is neither within nor without nature, any such void, but "Omnia Jovis plena," then we are in theism. There remained yet the middle way, which I took, which was to suppose that space was neither God, nor nothing but an attenuated form of matter. Have I the honour, or do you dispute it with me, of having invented this bold hypothesis? I own that I was at great fault how to make the first start in the evolution from this apparently non-entical void to that very substantial sun-dust of which the globes in our system are composed; but analogy helped me as it has helped the greatest philosophers. We do not see those great realities the souls of our fellow-creatures, and matter itself exists, in numerous instances, in an attenuated form, so as to be imperceptible to the senses.

Space then may be only attenuated matter, if only there were any proof that it is so; and the evolution into sun-dust is conceivable, if there were only anything to cause it. For why should our *Prima Materia* develope itself rather than remain eternally undeveloped?—Well, there must be, in every transcendental theory, many gaps and silent spaces. "The First Matter," I said, sheltering myself under a convenient phrase, as many of my philosophical brethren have often done,—"The First Matter developed itself by the law of its own nature;" but law—what is that? The existence of the attenuated matter is a *fact*, we will say; and law also is a fact; but is it not something more than a mere fact? Is it not the rule by which facts proceed? Can such a rule then be identical with the facts themselves? What furnishes the law of the development? The God whom we have excluded from the universe would help us here most opportunely. Shall we say, unless indeed the term be unmeaning, that the evolution is fortuitous? Now the term chance, in one sense at any rate is not unmeaning, it certainly means the opposite of law. It absolutely excludes law. But if the evolution be fortuitous how account for the fact of law? For not only is law a fact, but the only evolution I know of, or can conceive is through law. The flower lies thus or thus furled up in the germ, that it may thus or thus expand, like the juggler's barber's pole.

That is the plan of the evolution, and to plan is to proceed by rule or law. But if this be so the brains are, so to speak, at the wrong end, in our theory, and his godship is topsy-turvy. I must postulate an infinite Mind, aided by an infinite Hand, to devise and effect the inscrutable evolutions of the universe; and we are once more in theism.

The difficulty may be avoided or rather postponed, by starting from the other side and reversing the process of evolution. Instead of matter evolving God, it is God who evolves himself as matter. But in adopting this line of course we bid adieu to materialism. Instead of "Matter accounts for everything," it is "God," we now say, "who accounts for everything, by evolution." The Infinite unfolds himself as the Finite. This is that higher Pantheism which, rather than that dirt-philosophy, as it has been called, of materialism, has seduced certain finer intellects. But if neither Fichte, nor Schelling, nor Hegel, were able to render it intelligible, it is hardly probable that Proteus or myself should succeed any better. Aristotle had said, ages ago, that if there be *only one substance then contradictories must be reconciled.* And the whole Post-Kantian history of metaphysics furnishes an instructive comment on the Stagyrite's words. The Infinite, and the Finite, self and not self, mind and matter, cannot be predicated of the same thing, nor of one another. Fichte's theory met the difficulty on the threshold. There was only one absolute Ego, and the non-ego had to be explained away as an unreality, as a mere limitation of the activity of the Ego. Thus the same subject was at once the principle of furtherance and of hindrance, of activity and limitation. It was contradictory, and the theory had to be abandoned. Then Schelling tried to mend it. The Primum Philosophicum was neither Ego nor non-ego, but the substance which lay at the root of both, and which developed itself in one phrase as Ego, and in another as non-ego. But how could the same subject have contradictory attributes—especially, Proteus remarks, as the attributes are but the *modus essendi* of the subject? Then came Hegel's outrageous theory, which found in contradiction itself the very kernel of truth, identified *being* and *nothing* and brought philosophy into contempt: "You don't mean to say," said Lockhart to Sir William Hamilton, who proposed to write in the leading Review an article on German Philosophy, "You don't mean to say that you are going to introduce that d——d nonsense into this country." The title of the treatise in which Hegel introduced his extraordinary theory to the world was, "The identity of the identical and the non-identical," which words when Oken read, he said he knew not if he were standing on his head or his heels.

But into what subtleties have I rushed! forgetting that I was to deal with Proteus, not as a philosopher, but as a man of the world. I return to my theory of development.

After having developed the world out of sun-dust, I did not deal with the obscure questions of the origin of animal or vegetable life, but proceeded historically.

But now, considering the matter critically, I must make a long and doubtful pause before the appearance of the meanest anelid. Indeed it seems to me that there is a gulf between the animate and the inanimate; and to affirm that the one could become the other seems the sheerest contradiction. The most refined forms of matter I am acquainted with are magnetism and electricity. Observing various electrical experiments, the other day, I could not but reflect how utterly the veriest slave of law was this secret fluid, just as much as water or mercury, quite as mechanical and lifeless, shut off and turned on at the whim of the operator—utterly devoid of spontaneity. There is an abyss, I say, between such a substance and the little caterpillar that raises itself erect on its hinder legs superior to the law of gravitation. How can I either affirm the identity of the animate and inanimate or the development of one from the other, without identifying the identical with the non-identical, that "—— nonsense?" If I saw an experiment in which life was apparently created, as in the case of the *Acarus Crossii*, I could never be so simple as to suppose that it was *really* created out of matter—but I have said something to this purpose before.

Then there is another gulf—between *mind* and *matter*. If any man choose to say that *matter can think*, of course he is free to say it; but, for my part, I could not render the statement intelligible either to myself or another; nor did I ever see an attempt to render it intelligible, though nothing be easier than to speak of thought as "cerebration;" the substitution of words for ideas is a very common fault even in books of science.*

I flatter myself that I made the development of the rude man from the ape, and the civilised from the

* *Vide* Appendix.

savage, sufficiently plausible for a paper theory; but I wonder what old Waterton would have thought of it all, who protested that he would travel any distance to see the ape that *could even be taught to throw a stone!** But I will say no more on this subject, but pass to one of infinitely higher importance, the moral qualities of man.

You saw that I could get no higher morality out of our theory than the morality of convenience, nor a better Divinity than the *Times* newspaper. "Argue with me," you say, "like a man of the world." Then I suggest, that if any rascally knave should hint that, if Proteus be honest, that is only because he finds his account in being so, rather than the opposite, such a one would run the risk of a broken head! How can Proteus accept a philosophy which fails to account for the mere fact of Proteus himself? Nor will he, nor can he, nor does he, nor did he, ever accept it. The whole action that he has taken, in this question of the existence of God, only convinces me more and more of the real intensity of his belief. But Proteus believes in science and progress, and science and progress seemed at variance with Faith. Hence the present controversy, which is now finished (at least, the most important part of it) so far as I am concerned.

I have no doubt that I have committed many errors in the course of the argument, which Proteus will have the opportunity of exposing. As I have not kept

---

* I have it on the authority of an eye-witness that the apes at Gibraltar do sometimes throw stones. The lady who told me she had been pelted by them was surprised at my cross-questioning her as to the fact.—P.

copies of my letters, I fear I must have often repeated myself, a fault of that *old age* which is already beginning in me. I may even (though I tremble to think of it) have fallen into some contradictions!! Never mind. I did not take up my pen to get me credit as a philosopher, but to see if by any means I might help Proteus, for the sake of our youthful friendship, and the good that I always loved, and yet love in him. And so farewell. Affectionately yours,
AMADEUS.

LETTER XV.

PROTEUS TO AMADEUS.

Scepticism a disease of the soul. A cripple cured by fire. A picture of Hell. Wherein Proteus had been pleased, and wherein disappointed with Amadeus. The mutual relations of soul and body. A leaf out of Savarin's "Cookery Book." Proteus's hope of hereafter, not in the immortality of the soul, but in the resurrection of the body. The Dizzying thought of God. He concludes.

IT is time, dear physician, that I should give you news of your patient, and the effect of these your marvellous prescriptions, and in an especial manner that I should thank you for the zeal and care you have shown in his behalf, a care for which, alas, he has no fee to offer, not even the fee of an absolute cure. Your cripple cannot yet go forth from the temple walking and leaping and praising God; but at least he can testify to this that, listening to your words, he has many times been on the point of casting away his crutches, feeling that his feet and ancle bones were receiving strength. Even yet, it may be that a full result will follow, if not immediately, still on some more favourable day, and aided by happier circumstances. Balmes was after all right in describing scepticism as a disease of the soul; and mine has been sick, too long sick, for me to hope for more than a gradual recovery, unless indeed the cure be hastened on by accident. A story was told me once by Lord

Lytton, of his uncle Sir Henry Bulwer, who for some months fancied himself affected with paralysis of the limbs; and who refused to put foot to the ground, but was wheeled in a chair by his servant. At last, one day, the Rhone steamer, on which he was travelling caught fire; and the captain, having run the boat ashore, a plank was thrown out by which the passengers might land. The first person observed upon this new bridge, and stepping nimbly down, was Sir Henry. When fairly safe upon the shore, he remembered himself, and called to his servant, "Carry me, Forster." But it was too late. Forster refused to hear more of his master's folly; and Sir Henry had to walk, and he walked very well till the day of his death. Who knows but I too may be forced by fire, some day, to my feet?

In the meanwhile, fancy or no fancy, I am unable to move, at least not in the waking world of daylight and sound reason; though once or twice at night, when all the house has been still, my soul has seemed suddenly to sit up awake and listening. Not many nights ago, I awoke with an indescribable sense of mental anguish, during which I realised to the full the possibility of hell, apart from physical pain, anguish so intense that any suffering of the body would have been a relief. Indeed for the moment I was as though separated from my body, as well as separated by walls of darkness, from my fellow men. I was abandoned to myself as to an evil companion whom I loathed, and with none other, not even a devil, to hear my cries. Then I felt little indeed of a materialist, or of a philosopher of any sort, or in any sense of the word. I knew that God had me in his power; and that, without further apparatus of flames and racks and scourges, I was in a natural way tasting the reality of hell. I needed no devil to torment me, only myself. By daylight, however, and being in sound health, these terrors vanished.

> " Night dreams and terrors every one
> Like a flock of rooks at a farmer's gun."

And yet I could not laugh. I am an atheist, but of those " who tremble at the hour of death."

An atheist! why? Have you not, all this while, been showing me a God, a mind in the universe; and has your skill been of no avail? I hardly know what to answer. Perhaps I shall do best by telling you how each of your letters affected me; and you must bear with me, remembering that it is a sick man who is speaking to his physician, and of his own disease.

When then I got your first letter directly answering mine (your No. 2),* in which you cited Bode's law of mathematical proportion in the distances of the planets from each other and the sun, I saw that you understood my case, and I was delighted, arguing wonderful results from your course of treatment. I could not have borne to have been told by you as I have been by others, that my misery was altogether of my own devising, and my pain a mere nervous affection; that there was no obscurity in the heavens above me, and no chasm in the earth at my feet, but only an obliquity of the eye which refused to see, and of the heart which refused to take courage. No, you entered, as you say, the " Cavern of Despair," and explored it with me fairly, and whithersoever I went. For some days after receiving this first letter, I went

* Letter VII.

about like the blind man, restored to sight, who saw men as trees walking; only that I, on the contrary, saw, as it were, trees walking as men, matter suddenly informed with mind. Here was a proof, a geometric demonstration, and of the very kind for which I had been looking. I had suffered a scholar's mate in argument, but I felt no chagrin. I do not think that even the inaccuracy of the law, which I discovered on reference to my library,* diminished this impression; and I am still ready to say with you, " It is impossible that this can be the result of chance."

Then came your letters on evolution and the Darwinian creed, in which you wielded your own and Mivart's sword, and hewed Darwin to pieces before my eyes.† I looked on in wonder, and abandoned this Agag to you, and without regret. Evolution even you brought to my feet, the captive of your bow and of your spear, and we emasculated him between us and left him harmless henceforth for ever.‡ Your

---

* I find the following note, in my manual of astronomy :—"The planet Neptune is far from satisfying the empirical formula of Titius' (Bode's) law. Its distance, which should be represented by No. 388, is in reality only 300. The first number too, Mercury, is irregular, as it should be $1\frac{1}{2}$ and $5\frac{1}{4}$."—P.

† As Darwin seems to have taken no notice of Mivart's objections to his law, beyond acknowledging their force, I feel bound to consider that he admits them in his own mind. I was one of Darwin's first disciples; yet I abandon him.—P.

‡ That the doctrine of Evolution is true I still hold, and am glad to find myself in such good company as St. Augustine, and St. Thomas Aquinas. Nor do I, by evolution, merely mean the evolution of an idea, but the reality of blood relationship between ourselves and the brutes. It seems to me that nothing now but the strongest evidence could disprove the relationship. When we see two persons closely resembling each other, we suspect them to be related in blood; we make inquiries, and find that they are brothers. There is historical

letters on beauty and the instincts of the beasts came as the Prussians at Waterloo. The foe was already fled. I will not fight over again with you here the details of each day's work; though I shall have some notes to make on these too, before we have done; suffice it to say the victory was yours, and I acknowledged it without grudging; and forgiving you even your picture of my Matter-God, which you had drawn in jest, and which I recognise as the very monster with whom I had been living face to face.
He and I

> "Had known each other,
> Like a sister and a brother,
> Living in the same lone home
> Many years."

till "we had grown like two shadows, into one;" and evidence of the fact. Again when we see two persons, from the same part of the world, also closely resembling each other, we assume blood relationship, and find that they are of the same tribe. Here there is no historical evidence; but we *fairly* assume the fact. Again, it is reasonable to suppose that the whole human race is related. Surely antecedent probability then is in favour of our relationship with all the mammals, perhaps with all organised creatures. The fact that we do not know the exact law by which the changes have been produced is not conclusive against the change, for we have historical evidence that changes occur; and differences exist between blood relations. The facts of hybridism shew every stage of sterility between members of what are considered separate species. I think it quite likely that man might produce a hybrid with the ape; while on the other hand Count Gobineau, in his "Essai sur l'inégalité des races humaines," states roundly that the mixed offspring of blacks and whites in the West Indies is dying out in the fourth generation. Sterility need not appear at any particular stage. A mule, in the *jardin d'acclimatation*, some years ago produced a foal. I do not then abandon evolution because I abandon Darwin's exposition of its action. But I speak of its being emasculated, because it has been shewn by Mivart to have a method in its action. It is no longer a mere blind law of matter, and therefore is harmless in our argument.—P.

now you had cast out and slain this unclean god. See, I have buried him. He shall trouble us no more. Enough, I was in error. There is mind in matter; and it is not the mind of man; yet is it God?

You will forgive me if I say that, after such great commencements, your later letters were a disappointment to me, and doubly unexpected. You had still to prove that God rules the world,* and that He is just and merciful. For this you postulated a future life. You say for instance, "If this world be a scheme complete in itself, Proteus' objections" (as to the failure of justice in this life) "are unanswerable." On the other hand, you had to shew that there was a reasonable probability of a future life; and for this you postulated that God is just. For you say, "The argument of the unequal distribution of the goods and prizes of life, the wrongs which require redress, and the ills which demand compensation, is better perhaps than metaphysical proof, in which I might suspect some secret flaw." Surely it is a vicious circle, unworthy of the text books, to argue, "God is just because there is a future life. There is a future life

* I trust that I should not have been found wanting in the argument here, had I only distinctly understood what was required of me. In the thesis given me to prove, in the programme, that there exists "a personal God, just and merciful, who rules the world," I regarded the latter clause, "*Who rules the world,*" as merely ampliative of the former, that *there is a God*. For I did not think it was incumbent on me, supposing it once established that there is a God, to prove, *as a distinct thesis*, that He rules the world. The quality of His governance, as just and merciful, would indeed require proof, since Proteus objected on this score; but I considered that the fact of His governance was carried by the very nature of the conclusion as to His existence; since He was required as the account of an immense system, in actual working, liable, as we see in its several parts, to disorder and decay, and requiring a constant, providential, minute superintendence.—A.

because God is just."* That God is just, in this world, that He is merciful, in this world, that vice in this world is always punished, and virtue always rewarded, you have hardly maintained; and, as to a scheme of God's providence in the ways of the world, you say: "Life is, in its object, a state of training towards perfection." But perfection is not gained in this world; nor would there be any object in being perfect only to die. As to His mercy too, you admit that God lets the world alone now, because, if the world were governed by a system of interpositions, everything would be out of joint, and we ourselves only the worse off. You therefore clearly count on another life, in which to vindicate God's purposes of mercy and justice towards man. It is, then, of this other life that we must make sure, or at least, that we must secure a "reasonable probability."

Putting aside then the argument that God's justice demands a future life, (for God's justice itself lies

* This is indeed a vicious circle, as Proteus puts it; but then, I submit that it does not fairly represent my argument. To make a "circle" one must be *proving;* but, it is not I, but Proteus who is proving. When I say that, "if this world be a scheme complete in itself, the objections of Proteus would be unanswerable," I am only suggesting that the supposition of a Future State would blunt the edge of his argument against the justice of God, based on the frequent miscarriage of justice in this life. When, however, I do prove the existence of such a Future State, I certainly adduce the justice of God, as an argument practically stronger than metaphysical proof; but, on the other hand, when I had to prove the justice of God, I did not bring the Future State as a proof, but the fact that virtue, *in this life,* is distinctly rewarded, *as* virtue, and vice punished, *as* vice (Letter XII.); so that there is no circle.

But it is cold comfort to justify myself, either to myself or the reader; for I regard that as a poor argument, whatever be its intrinsic merits, *which does not convince Proteus.*—A.

trembling in our balance), you refer me only to the metaphysical arguments as to the nature of the soul ; and in them I find the very "secret flaw," * which you are already half prepared to suspect. All arguments of this sort err by assigning to the soul an undue share in each man's individuality, if they do not state in so many words that she is identical with that individuality. You yourself say "my soul is myself;" and in the next line, add, "my body is *mine*; it is not *I.*" Surely this is curiously illogical ; or why do we say *my* soul, if it is not mine ; and, if mine, how can it be I ? You would not tolerate me for a moment, if I were to reverse the dogma, and say, "my body is *myself;* my soul is *mine;* it is not I. Yet surely I have as good right to dogmatise as you have, that is to say, no right at all. I found the other day a passage quoted from Homer, to this effect: "The souls of these heroes went down to hell ; but they themselves αὐτοι, remained as a prey to dogs ;" which shows that, in Homer's mind at least, it was the body rather the soul which was " I." Which then is right, the heathen poet or the Christian philosopher ? I say without any hesitation "both and neither." Body and soul are the two sides of the shield ; and it is as true and as false to say of either side, " This is the shield, the other is only back," as it is to speak as you and Homer do. For my part I could not say otherwise, than that my body is mine and my soul is mine.

* When I used the words which have thus enabled Proteus to make a rhetorical point against me, I need hardly say, that I really suspected no such flaw as I said, " I might suspect ;" but only meant that I prefer *practical* proof, where it can be had to *metaphysical*, as in general, so in this particular instance.—A.

> " I am but by your union.
> With either soul or body lost
> All perishable. Then work ye on
> Together still not *corpse* and *ghost*.*

> " To live and be is a brave boast.
> Learn this ; alone, ye nothing can ;
> Yet, both together, ye make man ? "

These are the lines of a doggerel, which I made years ago, on the rival claims of soul and body; and in which I represented the body as coming into court with a petition against the soul. The soul was called upon to state her merits. She was one, indivisible, immortal, possessed of individuality. As a fact she ruled the body, making it go whithersoever she willed.

The body was her instrument, and she claimed him as her slave. Then the body spoke. If the soul was *one*,† he was *one* too. His individuality was as absolute as hers ; and, if she could survive the loss of parts, memory, reason, conciousness, so he survived the loss of arm and leg, and yet was no less the

---

* Common parlance helps us here. The living body and soul become, when dead, respectively corpse and ghost ; the man himself is "no more."—P.

† Surely there is unity, identity, individuality in a tree, though according to popular belief trees have no souls.—P.

It seems to me that there are *grades* of souls (why not, as there are grades of bodies ?) if I can only accurately state them. The lowest grade is that which has mere *spontaneity*—the vegetative soul. The grade above adds *sensation and intelligence* to spontaneity—the animal soul ; while the highest grade, the human soul adds *reason* (and with it freedom and responsibility) to intelligence, sensation, and spontaneity. But let not any one so misunderstand me, as to think that I am setting a brute or a plant on the level with mankind, merely because I say that it has a sort of soul.—A.

same body. If she ruled him by day, he ruled her by night.

> "She was wounded, and I wept;
> I was weary, and she slept."

In truth I cannot understand the distinction you make on this head. For my own part, looking back at what my soul was twenty years ago, and what my body, I find that my soul is the more changed of the two. In spite of its renewal of substance once in twelve years, I have the same freckles on my hand as I had when I was a boy, the same tricks and habits of body; but what a change in the tricks and habits of my soul! Have you never had dreams in which the soul was palpably the slave and instrument of the body! When I am cold at night I dream of beautiful scenery, and almost always the same dream; a little derangement of the stomach and what thoughts! As to the soul's immortality, Socrates was obliged to maintain that it had lived before its life in the world, in order to prove that it would live after it. But he gives no proof, beyond certain vague, aborted memories, in which, probably, neither you nor I believe at all. I have looked anxiously for signs of immortality in my own soul, and I find nothing there to suggest such a doctrine. When my body is weak, instead of my soul's gaining strength, she becomes weak too. I cannot think clearly when I am tired with playing tennis, though my soul has been all the day idle. My mind is more vigorous now than it was ten years ago; but then I enjoy better health. In old age the soul as often decays first as does the body. Generally both go together. Last of all death comes. Its approaches have wearied the body and wearied the mind. In extreme old age both flicker out together. What sign is there of immortality in this? *

There is a delightful story to our point in Savarin's Cookery Book, which I must transcribe. It is too pretty to mutilate; and I hold it to contain the germs of a great truth:

"J'avais une grande tante, âgée de 93 ans, qui se mourait. Quoique gardant le lit depuis quelque temps, elle avait conservé toutes ses facultés; et on ne s'était aperçu de son état qu'à la diminution de son appétit et à l'affaiblissement de sa voix.

" Elle m'avait toujours montré beaucoup d'amitié, et j'etais auprès de son lit, prêt à la servir avec tendresse; ce qui ne m'empêchait pas de l'observer avec cet œil philosophique que j'ai toujours porté sur tout ce qui m'environne.

"' Es-tu là, mon neveu?' me dit-elle, d'une voix à peine articulée.—' Oui, ma tante; je suis à vos ordres, et je crois que vous feriez bien de prendre un peu de bon vin vieux,'—' Donne, mon ami; la liquide va toujours en bas.' Je me hatai; et la soulevant doucement, je lui fis avaler un demi-verre de mon meilleur vin. Elle se ranima à l'instant; et, tournant sur moi des yeux qui avaient été fort beaux: 'Grand merci, me dit-elle, de ce dernier service; si jamais tu viens à mon âge, tu verras que la mort devient un besoin, tout comme le sommeil.'

---

* It was easy for Socrates, in the full vigour of his intellect, to refuse a belief that he must suddenly die. His body might die, but he cared little for that. He was the ugliest man alive; but he clung to his soul, for that was beautiful. Yet if he had lived to extreme old age, it would have been easier for him to relinquish both. Who that first saw the sun high over head, in its midday splendour, would dream that it must be blotted out that night?—P.

"Ce furent ses dernières paroles ; et demi-heure après, elle s'était endormie pour toujours."

I once sat by the death-bed of one whom I loved, and with whom I had walked step by step, through many months of pain, down all the valley of the shadow of death. He had no doubt whatever of a future life, and a firm trust in God; and it was his wont to speculate upon the particular form death would take with him, and on the thoughts which he should have, on entering another world. At last his hour came; but his soul was then already too weak to think; and, though for an instant he almost grasped the thought, yet it escaped him, and he passed away without knowledge of that which he was doing. As I sat beside him during the hour which followed his death, I could not think of him as one who still lived. His soul had died visibly before my eyes with his body. I could not believe in the immortality of the soul. Yet I live in the hope he held that he may rise again.

No : I have not a point of evidence that mind can be apart from matter, (even your proof of God does not goes so far as that); and, if we are to live again, it must be in accordance with the Christian doctrine of the resurrection of the body, and not with the Pagan theory of the soul's immortality.

What God it is whom you have shewn me in the universe, I know not. You have exposed to me the impossibilities of materialism, expose to me the possibility of God. I try in vain to picture to myself a beginning, a creation, a making of something where nothing was. The thought of God, in the midst of His Eternity, creating time, dizzies me. What point was there in Eternity, what day on which Time began? It is well to call these things mysteries, but to me they are impossibilities.* I think I might conceive an Eternal Mind in cöexistence with an eternal matter, as our temporal minds cöexist with our temporal bodies; but the thought of mind by

* Thus is the physic of one mind the poison of another! For the impossibilities of Proteus are arguments of my faith, I believe in a God who is incomprehensible; and it is just in such enigmas, that I am made to realise His incomprehensibility. "Methinks," says a quaint author whom I have quoted before,—"Methinks there be not impossibilities enough in religion for an active faith. . . . I love to lose myself in a mystery, to pursue my reason to an *O, altitudo!* . . . I can answer all the objections of Satan or my rebellious reason with that odd resolution I learned of Tertullian: *Certum est quia impossibile est!*" "Religio Medici," Bk. 1., 9.

Surely it is but the narrowness of our own minds which makes God seem strange to us. But, lest I seem to shirk difficulties which I cannot answer, I will make a few remarks on these supposed impossibilities.

1. The impossibility of God, *if He does not actually exist*, reminds me of an argument which I remember to have seen in the text-books, and which, though oddly stated, is by no means so absurd as it looks: "God is possible, therefore He exists: because, *if He did not exist He would not be possible.*" For my part, if there be evidence, in point of fact, that there is a God, I waive the question of His possibility.

2. Another impossibility is that of conceiving a point in eternity when Time began. As an illustration of this difficulty, Let the line A B., be supposed to be infinite, at both ends; and the point C, shall indicate the epoch in eternity when Time began.

    A   C   B

...━━━━━━━━━━━━━━━━━━━━━━━━━━━━━...

Now the portion of the line CB, is inexhaustible, on the hypothesis, can never run out. But suppose we travel backwards along the other portion of the line, CA, that is equally inexhaustible, for the same reason; because the line is infinite one way as the other. But if so *the point C. can never occur.* For, in order that it should occur, we must suppose Eternity *á parte ante* to have run out, which is equally against the hypothesis as to suppose that Eternity *á parte post* can run out.

I had always thought that this illustration was my own invention, until itself has no parallel, no symbol in Nature. Matter indeed we find alone, but mind nowhere. Believe me when I say I am still impotent to conceive the thought of God.

Such, dear Amadeus, are the diseases of your friend,

a friend pointed it out to me in WOODWARD'S SERMONS and ESSAYS, (*Ess.* ix.) Thus do our predecessors continually prevent us from being original! The author, moreover, makes the same use of it that I did myself, viz. ; to show that Time and Eternity are incommensurables, not only in degree, but in kind, For the fallacy of the reasoning consists in assuming that Eternity is only an indefinitely protracted Time ; whereas to apprehend Eternity one must transcend the notion of Time. For in Eternity, which is one abiding Now, there is neither *ante* nor *post*—neither Past nor Future. And so the question, "At what point in Eternity did Time begin?" becomes unmeaning. For Time is an attribute of the Creature only, not of the Eternal. And if this notion of Eternity seem unreal, yet the notion of Time seems to me even more unreal. Time is the standard measure of motion ; but a standard should be something *fixed*; whereas the hours and minutes of the clock, the vicissitudes of the heavenly bodies, or the thoughts in our mind, whereby we mete to ourselves the succession of events in Time, do themselves change and succeed to one another ! I want the notion of Eternity to clear my head of the illusions of Time, and learn the lesson of its nothingness.

3. That mind should exist without matter—the next impossibility of Proteus, is to me no impossibility at all, but rather that mind should ever be joined to matter. It seems I could quickly prove *à priori*, that such a mongrel creature as man, composed of soul and body, is more impossible than a centaur. The fact that I myself am such a being, when I reflect, does not decrease the wonder of it. How I came to be joined to a body, or how I can use it now I am joined to it, is as great a riddle to me as any in divinity. I do not know how it is that I can see or hear, or so much as lift a finger. The physiological analyses of the eye, or ear, or muscles do not help me here. They only begin where the mystery ends : they show me how I see, since I see, or hear, if I hear. That I shall one day die is no wonder. The wonder is that I live a single moment.

Thus surrounded with everyday experiences of things which in reason I can never understand, why should I be perplexed at the mysteries of the unseen world and of its Author?—A.

such his darkness, yet, compared with the past years, the days of his utter night, there is some glimmer, as of dawn. Sometimes he dreams that he can see; sometimes he almost hopes; but his soul is very weak. There are moments, nay days and weeks, when she seems incapable of ever caring to know the truth. I am afraid, if she could always find pleasure enough to her hand, she would be content, even now, with ignorance. The least amusement, while it lasts, shuts everything else out, and pleasure, sweet, palpable pleasure still fairly turns her head.

Fortunately these things are failing me, and I am in a sea of troubles:

> "We sometimes sit in darkness. I long while
> Have sat there, in a shadow as of death.
> My friends and comforters no longer smile,
> And they who grudge me wrongfully my breath
> Are strong and many. I am bowed beneath
> A weight of trouble and unjust reproach
> From many fools and friends of little faith.
> The world is little worth, yet troubles much.
> But I am comforted in this, that I,
> Although my face is darkened to men's eyes,
> And all my life eclipsed with angry wars,
> Now see things hidden; and I seem to spy
> New worlds above my heaven. Night is wise
> And joy's full sun-light never guessed the stars."

Yours affectionately, PROTEUS.

✲ The foregoing most touching letter of Proteus, exhibiting as it does a condition of soul which it belongs rather to grace than to argument to ameliorate, was never answered by Amadeus. Those matters in

it, however, which concern the questions of personality and immortality, demand some animadversion, since it would be equally unsatisfactory to the reader of the correspondence as to Proteus himself that a statement as to the relations of soul and body should pass unchallenged, which issues in the startling conclusion that *the soul dies together with the body!*

Now it may be admitted that the body enters more largely into the notion of personality than might appear from the psychological statement which Proteus condemns. That the body shares in the personality of man, is implied in the very union of the two natures. And if to wear a beard or not, to lose an eye or a tooth, even to put on a garment of another fashion, will oftentimes make a friend strange in one's eyes, and for a time to seem other than himself, how much more must the quality and condition of the bodily organs, temperament, and the modification of character induced by habit, manner of living, and a hundred other such influences, enter into the notion of personality?

Then there is to be considered the mutual action and reaction of soul on the body and body on the soul, of which Proteus makes so much, and which no psychologist can afford to underrate. All this is true. And if the metaphysician seems to forget it, when treating of personality, one obvious reason is, that it is his aim, not merely to determine in what consists the notion of personality, but to discover the root and account of such personality. Now a person is, strictly speaking, an individual; and whatever belongs to the person can only belong to him inasmuch as it shares in such individuality. While a man wears a coat, the garment seems for a time as it were a part of his person ; let him once cast it off and there is nothing personal about it. And so with the members of the body. Richard is Richard still, though he have lost an arm or a leg. While the limb remained to him, it was knit into his personality, by virtue of the individuality, which, so to speak, inflowed into it; but cut off from the individuality, it is like another lump of matter; it subsides into its constituent atoms, which have nothing more in common than so many pebbles. And the same is true, as of each member so of the whole body. How should this manifold become one, how is it one, but by the intimate pervading presence of one principle, which unites and holds together its several parts in sympathetic union ? And how can body and soul claim an equal share in the personality, seeing that it is the soul as an individual principle, which is the very source of personality. Then there is to be taken into account the significant fact that the soul uses the several organs of the body as instruments mechanically contrived ; by how much, surely, the power which uses is superior to the instrument used, by so much must the soul be conceived as superior to the body in the account of personality.

When, therefore, the metaphysician says (as all spiritualistic metaphysicians say), my body is mine, but my soul is myself, this statement must be understood, not indeed as denying that the body shares in the personality (it does so by the very fact of its union with the soul), but only as an emphatic affirmation that the root and account of personality is, not in the body but in the soul. And if it is true, as Proteus observes, that one sometimes says, "My soul is mine," surely this is only a fashion of speaking and allowable tautology; since it is the soul which possesses and uses the body, not the body the soul.*

And now as to the immortality of the soul. If the soul is individual, its destruction by death, which is nothing more than the dissolution of parts, is unmeaning. If the soul stands in relation to the organs of the body as an agent which uses their instrumentality, the destruction of the instrument does not involve the destruction of the agent. What shall be the manner of the soul's existence when death has dissolved the eye and the ear and the brain, until these be restored in the glorified state of corporeal resurrection is indeed a mystery; but such ignorance is no argument against the immortality of the soul, if otherwise established. And if the *mere* immortality of the soul, without regard of the body, be rather as Proteus objects, "a heathen notion," yet can he think that the statement that the soul dies together with the body is a Christian statement? For what on this hypothesis, becomes of the parable of Dives and Lazarus, conversing after death in an intermediate state? or

* In fact we can say, "*My* personal Principle," or "*my* Individual Being," as well as "*my* Soul;" and yet each of these expresses our absolute and essential EGO, as distinguished from all besides. But indeed the simple word "*my*" has a dozen meanings and different applications. In "*my* Personality" or "*my* Soul," it is used in an *absolute* sense; while "*my* Body" is the nearest of my possessions and the highest of my instrumentalities. "*My* property" is mine *legally;* "*my* country," *morally; my* worldly expectations, *prospectively; my* latent capacities, *potentially; my* repute, by imputation, conventionally, and comparatively.—ED.

how should "your father Abraham desire to see my day?" and yet, it is added, "he saw it and was glad."

But since Proteus adds that *he saw the soul of his friend die together with his body*, I can only say that I believe him; and that he really saw that which he saw. For sight is only of that which appears. Even so has he seen the sun die out of the world, and make it night; but only to shine elsewhere. But, as he speaks of his experience, let me speak of mine, which points to the very opposite conclusion :—

I have known a soul to be joined in companionship with a body that was practically dead—dead by almost every outward token of death. And they who wept and prayed around his bed, thought that the soul too was dead, or as good as dead; and spoke of him as of one already gone, who could not hear, or know what was doing around him. But, meanwhile, the soul lived, and waked, and heard, and knew; and wrestled with the body, which it could not move— no, not so much as a finger tip; nor could it speak, nor give a sign, the slightest even, to tell them how it fared with it. Then, one of the bystanders—though little hoping it could be of use — raised up the drooped head, and poured a cordial down the throat; shortly whereupon, the man of death groaned loud; and at last raised himself—it seemed like another Lazarus; and, shortly again, unglued his lips, and made his voice obey the will, and told the writer, how that his soul had waked, the while they spoke and wept and prayed; and how he heard and knew all that they said and did, and struggled against his corpse, which he could not govern to make a sign. Which rather was the *Person* here—the soul which waked and willed so ineffectually, or the moribund body? And which is rather to be apprehended—that the soul should cease together with the body, or that it should suffer, perchance, a horror like this man's, of being united to a body dead or moribund, and the spirit unable, quite at once, to cast the slough and escape?

When next I came they told me he was *dead.*— Dead! Were I the veriest heathen unbaptized, I could not believe that he was dead. But I saw the sallow mask, lying on the bed, where he had left it when at last he got away. AMADEUS.

APPENDIX.

EXTRACTS FROM
COLERIDGE'S "BIOGRAPHIA LITERARIA."

It is thus that Coleridge remarks upon Hartley's system of materialism.

"That thinking is a property of matter under particular conditions, is indeed the assumption of materialism, a system which could not but be patronized by the philosopher, if only it actually performed what it promises. But how any affection from without can metamorphose itself into perception or will, the materialist has left, not only as incomprehensible as he found it, but has aggravated it into a comprehensible absurdity. For, grant that an object from without could act upon conscious *Self*, as on a consubstantial object; yet such an affection could only engender something homogeneous with itself. Motion could only propagate motion. Matter has no *Inward*. We remove one surface but to meet with another. We can but divide a particle into particles; and each atom comprehends in itself the properties of the material universe. Let any reflecting mind make the experiment of explaining to itself the evidence of our sensuous intuitions, from the hypothesis that in any given perception there is a something which has been communicated to it by an impact, or an impression *ab extra*. In the first place, by the impact on the percipient or *ens representans*, not the object itself, but only its action, or effect, will pass into the same. Not the iron tongue, but its vibrations, pass into the metal of the bell. Now in our immediate perception it is not the mere power or act of the object, but the object itself, which is immediately present. We might indeed attempt to explain this result by a chain of deductions and conclusions, but that, first the very faculty of deducing and concluding would equally demand an explanation; and secondly, that there exists in fact no such intermediation by logical notions, such as those of cause and effect. It is the object itself, not the product of a syllogism, which is present to our consciousness. Or would we explain this supervention of the object to the sensation, by a productive faculty set in motion by an impulse, still the transition, into the percipient, of the object itself, from which the impulse proceeded, assumes a power that can permeate and wholly possess the soul.

> ' And like a God by spiritual art
> Be all in all, and all in every part.'

And how came the percipient here? And what is become of the wonder-promising Matter, that was to perform all these marvels by force of mere figure, weight, and motion?' . . . 'Thus, as Materialism has been generally taught, it is utterly unintelligible, and owes all its proselytes to the propensity so common among men, to mistake *distinct images* for *clear conceptions;* and, *vice versa*, to reject as inconceivable whatever from its own nature is *unimaginable*. But as soon as it becomes intelligible it ceases to be materialism. In order to explain *thinking*, as a material phenomenon, it is necessary to refine matter into a mere modification of intelligence, with the twofold function of appearing and perceiving. Even so did Priestley in his controversy with Price. . . . He stripped matter of all its material properties; substituted spiritual powers; and when we expected to find a body, behold! we had nothing but its ghost, the apparition of a defunct substance."—*Biographia Literaria*, vol. I. part ii., pp. 134 to 139. Edit. 1847.

Coleridge assigns another reason for the tendency to materialistic views, shewn occasionally by minds the reverse of materialistic. "The attention will be more profitably employed in attempting to discover and expose the paralogisms, by the magic of which such a faith could find admission into minds framed for a nobler creed. These, it appears to me, may be all reduced to one sophism as their common *genus;* the mistaking the conditions of a thing for its causes and essence; and the process by which we arrive at the knowledge of a faculty for the faculty itself. The air I breathe is the condition of my life, not its cause. We could never have learned that we had eyes but by the process of seeing; yet, having seen, we know that the eyes must have pre-existed in order to render the process of sight possible."—*Ibid.* p. 126.

Again he remarks, "under this strong sensuous influence we are restless because invisible things are not the objects of vision; and metaphysical systems, for the most part, become popular, not for their truth, but in proportion as they attribute to causes a susceptibility of being seen, if only our visual organs were sufficiently powerful."—*Ibid.* p. 113.

Coleridge indicates with no less discernment the consequences, which in strict logic would follow from Materialistic Principles, viz. the cessation of any real belief either in Man, or in God. He says:—"According to this hypothesis, the disquisition to which I am at present soliciting the reader's attention, may be as truly said to be written by St. Paul's Church as by me; for it is the mere motion of my muscles and nerves; and these again are set in motion from external causes equally passive, which external causes stand themselves in interdependant connection with everything that exists, or has existed." ... "The same must hold good of all systems of philosophy; of all arts, governments, wars by sea, or land; in short of all things that ever have been, or that ever will be produced. For, according to this system, it is not the affections and passions that are at work, in as far as they are sensations or thoughts. We only fancy that we act from rational motives, or from impulses of anger, love, or generosity. In all these cases the real agent is a *something-nothing-everything*, which does all of which we know, and knows nothing of all that it does." Next he shews the bearings of materialistic views on Theism. "The existence of an Infinite Spirit, of an Intelligent and Holy Will, must on this system be mere articulated motions of the air. For as the function of the human understanding is no other than merely to appear to itself to combine, and to apply the *phenomena* of the association; and as these derive all their reality from the primary sensations; and the sensations again all their reality from the impressions *ab extra;* a God not visible, audible, or tangible, can exist only in the sounds and letters that form his name and attributes." . . . "Very far am I from burdening with the odium of these consequences, the moral characters of those who first formed, or have since adopted this system." . . . "So true is it that the Faith, which saves and sanctifies, is a collective energy, a total act of the whole moral being; that its living *sensorium* is in the heart; and that no errors of the understanding can be morally arraigned unless they have proceeded from the heart. But whether they be such, no man can be certain in the case of another, scarcely perhaps even in his own." . . . "It does not however by any means follow that opinions fundamentally false are harmless. A hundred causes may co-exist to form one complex antidote; yet the sting of the adder remains venomous, though there are many who have taken up the evil thing, and it hurted them not."—*Ibid.* p. 122, 4, 5.

These remarks of Coleridge have an important bearing on the preceding Correspondence. No thoughtful man who has once come to see clearly that all the higher processes, and more creative energies, in his own being, proceed from something more than his material nature, can rest content with the belief that, externally to himself, there exists nothing but matter. He is almost irresistibly drawn to the conviction that the material Universe owes its origin to a Creator eternal and spiritual—a Father of Spirits, immeasurably greater and wiser than his own spirit.

A. DE VERE.

www.ingramcontent.com/pod-product-compliance
Lightning Source LLC
Chambersburg PA
CBHW020906230426
43666CB0C008B/1335